HOPEDALE REMINISCENCES

Hopedale Reminiscences

Childhood Memories of the Hopedale Community and the Hopedale Home School 1841-1863

Edited by Lynn Gordon Hughes

 Blackstone Editions
Providence

Blackstone Editions, Providence, Rhode Island 02906
Published 2006. Reissued 2015
Printed in the United States of America

ISBN-10: 0-9725017-4-6
ISBN-13: 978-0-9725017-4-3

Editor's Preface © 2006 by Blackstone Editions

"Hopedale" by William F. Draper is an abridgement of chapters 1 and 2 of William F. Draper, *Recollections of a Varied Career* (Boston: Little, Brown, and Company, 1909).

"Memories of the Hopedale Home School" and "Catalogue of the Hopedale Home School" are adapted from *Home School Memorial: A Reunion of Teachers and Pupils of the Hopedale Home School, at Hopedale, Milford, Mass., August 1, 1867; to which is added a complete catalogue of the members of that institution* (Cambridge, MA, 1867).

The remaining chapters are from *Hopedale Reminiscences: Papers Read before the Hopedale Ladies' Sewing Society and Branch Alliance, April Twenty-Seventh, Nineteen Hundred and Ten* (Hopedale, 1910). Spelling and punctuation have been modified slightly. The extracts from the *Practical Christian* in "Christmas in the Old Days" have been restored to the form in which they originally appeared in the *Practical Christian*.

Contents

Editor's Preface	vii

HOPEDALE REMINISCENCES (1910)

The Old House of Hopedale *Sarah L. Daniels*	1
Community Life as Seen by One of the "Young People" *Sarah E. Bradbury*	10
The Post Office *Susan Thwing Whitney*	13
Anti-Slavery and Other Visitors to the Community *Anna Thwing Field*	17
Recollections of Hopedale *Ida D. Smith*	22
Reminiscences of the "Home School" and the Village *Imogene Mascroft*	27
The Burglary *Susan Thwing Whitney*	31
Our Community School and its Teacher *Ellen M. Patrick*	33
Christmas in the Old Days *Frank J. Dutcher*	36

Childhood Days in the Hopedale Community, and Other Recollections *Nellie T. Gifford*	42
Hopedale Community, Founded in 1841: Its Origin and Early History *Abbie Ballou Heywood*	48

RECOLLECTIONS OF A VARIED CAREER (1909)

Hopedale *William F. Draper*	61

HOME SCHOOL MEMORIAL (1867)

Memories of the Hopedale Home School *Retrospective Sketch* *Address by the Orator of the Day* *Response to Toast "To the Principals of the Home School"*	69
Catalogue of the Hopedale Home School	74
ILLUSTRATIONS	85

Editor's Preface

The Hopedale Community, established in Milford, Massachusetts in 1841, was one of the most successful of the many communitarian experiments initiated in the 1840s. Under the spiritual leadership of the Universalist minister and social reformer Adin Ballou, the members of the Community sought to live together, sharing what they had, and removing themselves, as much as possible, from dependence upon harmful and coercive force. Thus they would have nothing to do with any government that executed criminals, waged war, or controlled its citizens with the threat of injurious force. Their religion, and their whole way of life – embracing non-resistant pacifism, moderate socialism, egalitarianism, liberal theology, and a life of purity and simplicity – they called Practical Christianity. By following its tenets they hoped both to find shelter from the "wicked world" and to serve as a model for a reformed order of society. In the words of the Community poet, Abby Hills Price, they prayed, "Earth's bitter founts of woe soon may we close, Making this world below bloom as a rose."

From its beginning as a "unitary household" of twenty-eight people sharing an old farmhouse, Hopedale grew over the next fifteen years into a busy little village of nearly three hundred people, engaged in farming and gardening, printing and publishing, crafts and light manufacturing – all the while adhering with reasonable fidelity to the tenets of Practical Christianity. Despite numerous attempts, however, the Community never succeeded in finding the perfect balance between individual and communal ownership. In 1856, the balance tipped decisively in the direction of private enterprise, and the experiment in Christian socialism came to an end. The Hopedale Home School, an academy and college preparatory school under the direction of Ballou's daughter and son-in-law, survived until 1863. Adin Ballou, hoping to benefit future generations, spent the remainder of his long life trying to understand what went wrong. He finally concluded that, though the Community had many successes, ultimately "we lacked the wisdom, the grace, the large-mindedness, the generosity, the nobility of soul" necessary for so great an endeavor.

After the dissolution of the Community, there must have been many who, like Ballou, reflected long and hard on the effort, the eventual failure, and the meaning of it all. However, more than fifty years passed before an organized effort was made to collect their stories. By that time, most of those who had been adults in the 1840s and 1850s had passed away, leaving the story to be told by people who had been children during Community days. The result was a unique child's-eye view of Community life. Their stories – eleven short pieces, written by nine women and one man who had been children in the Hopedale Community or students in the Hopedale Home School – were published as *Hopedale Reminiscences: Papers Read Before the Hopedale Ladies' Sewing Society and Branch Alliance, April 27, 1910.*

For anyone interested in understanding the nature and significance of the Hopedale Community, *Hopedale*

Reminiscences is essential reading, along with Adin Ballou's *History of the Hopedale Community* (1897). The variety of voices and viewpoints in the *Reminiscences* reminds us that the Community was not just the lengthened shadow of Adin Ballou, but the joint creation of all of its members: male and female, old and young.

In some ways, children make ideal guides for a trip into the heart of Hopedale. As childhood memories often do, the *Reminiscences* preserve homely details that an adult might not have considered worthy of mention: meals of cornmeal mush and milk, a red cloak made out of an old ball dress, a sunny landing half-way down the stairs, the moldy smell of the pantry, the names of the oxen and horses. Only a child would remember making a playhouse under Adin Ballou's desk, or being taken to Boston to see trained seals and mice, or raising $2 to buy shoes for the poor children of Milford.

The adults of Hopedale, for whom the Community was the embodiment of a powerful urge to re-create society on a new foundation, could have told us about their intentions, hopes, fears, and disappointments; but the intensity of their desire for reform must inevitably have colored their perceptions of the world they made. Only the children, bobbing along in their parents' wake, were in a position to observe this world closely yet dispassionately. They could honor the Hopedale pioneers for their "faith, zeal, and determination," their courage and generosity, their earnest efforts to overcome evil and live in peace. But they could also see the silly side of a community in which tongues wagged when a woman wore flowers in her bonnet; in which "to shave or not to shave was a burning question"; and in which impassioned debates over phrenology and spiritualism, dress and diet made Community meetings "a 'continuous performance' of vast entertainment." A century and a half later, we can giggle and roll our eyes along with these young people, even as we join their grown-up selves in mourning the passing of a generation of reformers "earnest and conscientious in their devotion to convictions of duty, whatever its cost and penalties."

In this volume, the *Hopedale Reminiscences* collected in 1910 are accompanied by sketches of childhood in Hopedale taken from two other sources: the chapter on Hopedale from William F. Draper's autobiography, *Recollections of a Varied Career* (1909); and *Home School Memorial*, the commemorative booklet produced on the occasion of the reunion of the Hopedale Home School in 1867. We have also included the "Catalogue," or list of the students and teachers of the Hopedale Home School, which was printed in the *Home School Memorial*.

William F. Draper was the son of George Draper, the man who is often cast as the villain (or hero, depending on your point of view) in the story of the transformation of Hopedale from utopian community to company town. Despite his family's complicated relationship with the Community, and his own aversion to socialism of any kind, William Draper's memories are surprisingly similar to those of the other children of Hopedale. Like the other children, he loved his school and his teachers, took pride in his work in the Community shops, and listened with interest to the lectures and debates at the Lyceum. He is forthright about the less attractive side of Community life – the endless debates over reform in some of its more cranky manifestations, and the petty tyranny of public opinion in matters of clothing and household furnishings – but no more so than Sarah E. Bradbury, Ida D. Smith, or even Abbie Ballou Heywood.

What makes Draper's memoir particularly valuable is the glimpse it provides of Hopedale from a boy's perspective – a much-needed supplement to *Hopedale Reminiscences*, since the only male contribution to the *Reminiscences* is Frank Dutcher's piece on the community's Christmas celebrations. It is only here, for example, that we hear of the special temptation facing the boys of the non-resistant community, who had to endure "opprobrious epithets," and worse, from the boys of Milford.

The *Home School Memorial* includes a brief history and description of the school and its educational philosophy – interesting enough in itself, but doubly so when coupled with extracts from the speeches given at the reunion. For while the "Retrospective Sketch" tells of the school's mission "to develop and establish pure, virtuous exalted characters – thus moulding and confirming the noblest types of Christian manhood and womanhood," the speeches recall "our insane desire to do that which was forbidden, as well as our earnest desire to do our duty."

Indeed, by all accounts the children of Hopedale were rambunctious, to say the least. The *Memorial* tells of using chairs as footballs, of raiding the principal's molasses barrel to make candy, and of the use of that most fearsome of childish weapons: the ridicule and contempt of the "principal young ladies" of the place. In the *Reminiscences* and in Ballou's *History of the Hopedale Community*, we read of the "rude and uncouth" manners of the children; of "lawless ways and growing disrespect of proper authority" on the part of the older boys; of profanity, vulgarity, obscenity, bullying, and fighting.

All this is perhaps to be expected; after all, the children, unlike their parents, were not a self-selected group with a pre-existing commitment to the ideals of the community. Yet the Home School and its predecessors, the Hopedale Juvenile Home School founded by Mr. and Mrs. Morgan L. Bloom and the Hopedale district school under the direction of "Mrs. Abbie" Ballou Heywood, did largely succeed in the moral education of their unruly charges. The secret of their success seems to have been a combination of meaningful work connected with the students' own life goals; the teachers' genuine concern and affection for the children in their care; and the entire community's unwavering confidence in the young people's ability to grow into highly responsible adults.

The educational programs at Hopedale reflected Adin Ballou's optimism, born from his Universalist faith, that everyone could achieve goodness. Ballou loved children, he enjoyed them, he respected them; he expected each one to succeed, and he rejoiced when they did. And that, in the end, is what they remembered about their Hopedale education.

The Old House of Hopedale

Sarah L. Daniels

In America there are few dwellings whose history dates back over 150 years, their builders constructing on such firm foundations, as to endure for so long a period the daily tread of the many feet that crossed their thresholds, as one family after another entered and departed from their doors. The Old House of Hopedale was one of this number. From the raising of its walls to the tearing apart of its timbers, it sheltered a multitude of souls, notably a good class of honorable people.

To review its history, before it became antiquated enough to receive the name of Old House, and after its occupancy as such, is a pleasurable task, as it was the early home of my childhood.

The years in Massachusetts following King Philip's War, in 1676, were followed by the return of settlers to their homes, having been driven away by the Indians who had destroyed their property.

John Jones came as a new settler, about the year 1700, to make a home on the banks of the Mill River in a section called The Dale, now Hopedale. His family was left behind in a distant town. With his axe over his shoulder, alone with his dog, he made daily trips over the Mendon hills to hew out of the forest timbers for a barrack, that he might be secure from roving Indians and wild beasts.

Bears, wolves, and panthers were then numerous enough to shorten his day's work, and he returned before dusk to the settlement he left in the morning. Faith in a kind Providence sustained him through all the trials of a pioneer life. He knelt in prayer before each frugal meal, believing that an over-ruling power protected him. Later on, behind the walls of his stockade, he remained all night, lengthening out his days.

This enclosure was built on the banks of the river, on Water Street. As late as 1805, it is related, that workmen unearthed the hearthstone of the old barrack, its embers having been preserved for a century.

About three years after his axe struck the first blow, his wife and five children joined him, he having prepared a small house for them. Prospering in later years, he added valuable parcels of land to his estate, and finally completed a fine mansion, unequalled by any other in the vicinity, and destined, years after, to be called The Old House.

John Jones was a very pious man. For many years he was an Elder in the First Church of Mendon. Finally, a new church was organized, as the people living at The Dale, and easterly, considered it a hardship to climb the Mendon hills.

Jones was chosen to fill the position of Elder in the new church, called the Second or Easterly Precinct Church of Mendon. It was situated on Sherborn Road, now Main Street.

The services attending the election of Officers of the Church were held in the Mansion house of Elder Jones. Its dining room, with a seating capacity of fifty guests, must have had, on this occasion, its long tables loaded with the profusion of country hospitality.

Reverend Amariah Frost was ordained pastor in 1743. For forty-nine years he ministered to the spiritual wants of his little flock, dying in 1792, at seventy-two years of age. (He married, for his third wife, Sarah Thwing, granddaughter of Elder Jones, an ancestor of Susan Thwing Whitney.)

The children of Elder Jones, sooner or later, became members of the Church. After marriage, they moved elsewhere, with the exception of the youngest son Joseph, who was associated with his father in the management of the estate. Elder Jones died in 1753, being over eighty years of age.

From an humble pioneer, striking out alone in the forest in his early manhood, he subdued the wilderness around him, and from the rich meadows of The Dale, his cattle brought him increase of wealth, until he became a landed proprietor. He had a family of nine children; they, with their grandchildren, inheriting the estate.

After the death of Joseph Jones in 1796, at the age of 87, the property was rented by the heirs for some time. My mother's uncle, Elisha Daniels, lived in the place for some years, dying there in 1821. His widow and children continued to reside there. The eldest son, Hastings, finally bought the place. After his death in 1839, the family left for Milford.

My mother's visits to the old homestead were frequent, when a young woman. The hospitality of her uncle's home was proverbial. Tradition tells of Washington's visit there on one occasion.

In 1841, the property was purchased as a site for the Hopedale Community. I was then a child of two years when my father, Henry Lillie, and wife took up their abode in the Old House, previous to the coming of other members of the Community. In October 1841 my sister Lucy was born.

Hers was the honorable distinction of being the first child born in the Hopedale Community. She was named Lucy Ballou Lillie, for the beloved wife of Reverend Adin Ballou.

The winter was a memorable one to my mother, for it was her first experience of frontier life. Being a very timid woman, she suffered exceedingly. From the back roads leading from Mendon, there often appeared wandering, dissolute men, who in those days were called "Shacks." On one occasion, father happened to be away, and a "shack" made his appearance, frightening us all with his peculiar actions. He drew out a long knife from his belt and commenced to sharpen it. No harm resulted therefrom, but we were glad to see him leave.

One family after another came in the course of a few months, and Community life began in earnest. Families were crowded, each into one room, which served as sleeping room, dining room, and kitchen.

My parents occupied the southeast chamber, a pleasant room with four windows. The bed was an old-fashioned four-poster, in summer curtained with mosquito netting. A trundle-bed underneath held the two youngest children, my sister and me.

On the upper floor was a large attic which was divided into two rooms, one of which was occupied by the older girls of the various families, the other by the boys.

The history of those old attic rooms would be an account of delightfully good times, the girls enjoying themselves especially, with credit to their memory. I have heard that some of the pranks the boys used to play on each other frequently went beyond the limit of decent behavior.

There was still another attic, one over the kitchen which was filled with odds and ends, such as we read about.

I remember the fragrant smell of herbs as the door opened. There were bunches of pennyroyal, sage, catnip and peppermint hanging with downward heads. Sassafras root and sweet-flag were bundled away in safe corners. Old trunks were there, with the ballroom dresses of my mother's dancing days, later on to be utilized for Sunday wear for her little girls. I remember that one gown, with its ample skirt, clothed us like Red Riding Hood. Resplendent in bright hues, with hoods and cloaks alike, we must have illumined our snowy pathway to Church.

This attic held another memory dear. As a child I was very fond of pets. I remember it as a place of refuge from my boy tormentors, who delighted to tease me and my kittens. The mother cat seemed also to know the safety of this place, for here, year after year, she raised her families undisturbed.

Down the back stairs, from the second floor, was a halfway landing before a window. This was a favorite corner for our dolls and their housekeeping arrangements. At the foot of the stairs was a hall with an outside door, and doors leading into the east room and the long dining hall. Here the Community table was spread and as it was filled with the gathered crowd, the number often reached fifty or more. The cooking was done by the women, who took turns, so many for a given period. My mother, who thoroughly enjoyed catering to a crowd, prided herself, when it came her turn to superintend, to give them all something extra good to eat. When some others, with less experience than she, had charge, oftentimes all the family had for supper was cornmeal mush and milk.

From the dining room opened a large pantry with its little window. I well remember its many drawers, shelves, and little cupboards, and especially the musty, moldy smell as the doors swung backward. The storage of food therein for more than a hundred years had permeated the wood with an odor that no washing could remove.

The kitchen was an ell, perhaps the original house built for the Jones family. The main part of the Old House, that afterwards received the name of Mansion, was not built until 1735.

One great feature of kitchens in olden times was a set kettle, so called because it was a kettle of huge dimensions set around with brick, with a place for a fire underneath. Here the clothes were boiled and, unless there was another for farm purposes, the chicken and hog feed were prepared, grease tried out after hog-killing, and water boiled for various purposes. Such a kettle was cornered in our kitchen. Stretched out at right angles from the ell was a long shed building. A bakery was established in one end, and a man was employed to bake the bread, pies, gingerbread, and beans and meat for the large family. A fire was kindled in the big oven. When thoroughly heated, the coals were withdrawn, and it was then ready for use. Beyond the bakery, connecting was the woodshed of immense capacity.

Returning to the dining room, a door opened therefrom to the cellar stairs. A black hole at the bottom I well remember, without ventilation, I imagine, as the house had an embankment of earth all around to keep out the frost. A candle was necessary even in daylight to penetrate its gloom. In one corner was a room with shelves for milk. A dining hall door opened into the north room, and here was a corner wainscot cupboard with glass paned doors in front and closet underneath. I imagine the china of the Jones family and later that of Uncle Daniels would be of treasured value now. I remember the porringers of pewter that were kept in this cupboard. They were low dishes with bulging sides with side handles, each containing about a pint, being a favorite dish in use for bread and milk.

I remember how badly my mother felt, years after, when Bridget turned one over and used it as a stand for her flat-iron, melting it all out of shape – and this, the last one.

Great oaken beams stretched across the ceiling of each room. Swings for the children were often upheld by them.

The four large rooms in the house bad each four windows with small panes of glass. Smaller rooms were on the upper floor in the rear. The outside door, midway between the two front rooms, opened into a long narrow hall. Underneath the front stairway was a closet, from the interior of which could be seen the immense stone chimney, built in the middle of the house from it foundations. Huge fireplaces in the large rooms opened into it.

In the front yard stood two large lilac trees, reaching to the chamber windows, on either side. On the north side were two flourishing elms.

From a gentle slope on the north end of the house, stone steps led into the garden. I suppose all sorts of vegetables were planted there in season. I remember most distinctly a fine large cherry tree that bore delicious fruit.

The old barns in front of the house were my delight. Wagon sheds to the left, the oxen and cows were stabled in the middle, and the horses to the right. Of the names of horses, so familiar then, only one is now remembered, that of Pompey. The happy days of memory that stood out from the rest were those when we drove with father and mother to visit one of our many aunts in an adjoining town, the only discord on such occasions being caused by the irritation of my father, who was constantly reminded by my mother of his inattention to his horse, her timidity preventing her from enjoying our ride.

One of the first schools of the Community was opened in an upper room of a building, whose lower part was used for a shop. The entrance was from outside stairs.

Rev. Adin Ballou was the teacher. I was so young at that time, that all I remember of my school days then was a reprimand that I received, with another little girl, for fastening a shawl around a tall desk in the room, making for ourselves a play-room. I think this must have been the same tall desk that I remember of seeing in his home years after, before which he either sat or stood, writing page after page of matter, so instructive and entertaining to his hearers.

A squabble with Abby Lucy Ballou, daughter of Amos Ballou, who was inclined to be belligerent as myself, was probably the cause of my withdrawal from school. Mrs. Amos bore down heavily upon me in the midst of our tussle, my mother over-looking from an upper window.

Knowing from long experience as a teacher that quarrels often arise between parents on account of their children, I suppose my mother thought I was the injured party, and if taken from school would no longer come in contact with Abby Lucy and her mother.

When I returned to school in the Spring, my mother was highly complimented by the Reverend Adin Ballou, as he considered my progress in reading under her instruction most satisfactory. Her reply to him firmly impressed itself upon my mind, when I was old enough to appreciate its merit.

Her plan was to teach each lesson so thoroughly, before going to the next, that the words therein could not be easily forgotten. This method must have left its impression, for during many years of teaching, I too received many compliments for instruction given in Reading.

During our several years of residence in the Old House, as a family, we came in contact with many singular people. Their peculiarities were indelibly stamped upon my young mind, assisted by the recollections of relatives.

The greater number of them, nearly all of my own family included, have left the world they tried so hard to benefit. I trust their efforts will be more and more appreciated as the spirit of reform permeates society generally. The principles of Christian Brotherhood they advocated are not dead. They are imperishable as the world itself.

Greenville, Sonoma County, California

Community Life as Seen by One of the "Young People"

Sarah E. Bradbury

After the reading of Mrs. Whitney's paper on the Inductive Communion of the Hopedale Community, a member of one of the old families, born too late to have known Community life, exclaimed with deep conviction, "How dreary those days must have been!" The conviction, though natural from an up to date point of view, was not true of the time referred to.

The members were men and women drawn together by a common interest in the great principles of liberal and practical Christianity at a time when church doctrines were narrow. In addition to the vital principles of ultimate salvation for all, temperance, non-resistance, etc. each one brought some fad of his own – a belief in Spiritualism, or the vegetable diet. Some were non-shavers, and all, I think, were non-smokers. The fads, which were almost as dear to the hearts of their owners as the principles, were often discussed in public, and the free play of the various natures, grave and gay, matter of fact and mischievously humorous, made these meetings a "continuous performance" of vast entertainment. The argument was earnest on either side, and usually closed by each with the same emphatic utterance, "So it seems to me and I cannot see it otherwise!" Neither party convinced the other, but the war of words afforded a certain relief to strenuous natures who, as good non-resistants, could indulge in no other form of warfare.

The small band of vegetarians were firm in the faith and provided much amusement for those who had no scruples against a meat diet. A wag among the latter having discovered that Mr. Asaph Spaulding, one of the most voluble defenders of vegetarianism, had fallen from grace by partaking of codfish, charged him with it in open meeting. Mr. Spaulding being for once at a loss for words, his wife came to the rescue, exclaiming, "Asaph wanted a codfish and I got him one!" On another occasion a young man who wished to deal fairly by both sides of the question, remarked that one's occupation should be considered in the matter of diet, and that the performance of manual labor required meat.

To shave or not to shave was a burning question. I remember a non-shaver who, having worked his fiery way to the climax, exclaimed, "I have not shaved for five years, and I never will shave again!" Instantly the quiet voice of Mr. Swazey answered, "You may get shaved though."

We young people had great enjoyment in what we called music, and at least one evening of the week was devoted to singing under the direction of Mr. W. W. Cook, or Mr. Hatch, and our unskilled performances gave great pleasure at the frequent picnics and festivals.

We were especially happy in our school under the inspiring teaching of Miss Abbie Ballou, afterwards Mrs. William S. Heywood. Her methods were in advance of those in use at that day, and the excellence of the little Hopedale district school attracted the attention of William Lloyd Garrison, C. F. Hovey and Samuel May, who each sent sons to receive the benefit of Mrs. Heywood's instruction. All who came under her influence in the old schoolhouse must feel that their lives had a fortunate beginning.

We children shared the feeling of our parents that we were a chosen band, safely sheltered from the wicked world. Milford, our nearest point of contact, was as remote as Boston seems to-day, and was perhaps more seldom visited. It was a long way off around by the road, and the short cut lay through woods and over rocky pastures. Mr. Bailey brought the mail over every evening by the latter route. I lived where I could see him emerge from the woods, on what is now Dutcher Street, and when the night was wild, he seemed to my fancy a veritable hero.

Community life was for children a simple and happy one. But later when, it became necessary to take a practical view of things and lower our standards to those of the ordinary business village, the charm dissolved – life became commonplace, and glimpses of the here-to-fore "wicked world" were eagerly sought by the young people.

Arlington, Massachusetts

The Post Office

Susan Thwing Whitney

Had you chanced to be in Hopedale fifty years ago, or a little earlier, you might have seen a chubby, rosy girl, with brown eyes and hair, who, every evening, except Sunday, between seven and eight, traveled over that part of Hopedale between Hope Street and the Corner. It was not Patrick's Corner then.

If you had happened to meet this little girl some stormy evening in winter, you could have seen that she wore a warm hood, rubber boots and leather mittens. In one hand she carried a lantern, a queer four-sided lantern, three sides of which were of glass and the fourth side had a handle to carry it by, and would also open, so the lamp could be taken out to be filled with whale-oil. In the other hand she carried a carpet-bag from which she took sometimes a letter and sometimes a paper, which she left in a house nearby.

So, allow me to present to you, Susie Thwing, one of the first mail carriers of Hopedale. The other carrier, whose route was the upper part of the village, was Anna Thwing, her sister.

When the Community was first started, the mail for Hopedale was brought from the Milford Post Office by anyone who happened to go there. About 1853, when Appendix A of the Constitution of the Community was written, Enactment 8 provided for establishing a Post Office in Hopedale. Soon after, my mother, Mrs. Almon Thwing, was elected Post Mistress. All mail leaving Hopedale was carried to my father's, who lived where Mrs. Charles M. Day's house is.

The letters were counted and securely locked in a bag, which was carried to the Milford Post Office by Mr. Pliny Southwick, or whoever drove the "express" to and from the railroad station. There were two mails daily, each way. The first arrived here in the middle of the forenoon, and the other, about half past six in the afternoon, but the carriers were only on duty after the latter.

Some of the older residents will no doubt remember the sign, "Letter Box," over a hole cut in the south side of my father's house, where the mail could be dropped into a box in the woodshed.

To pay for the work of carrying and caring for the mails, a little stamp was issued which cost the sender or receiver of a letter, living in Hopedale, one and one half cents. The first issue was a pink, oblong stamp, about an inch long, and the second was square and yellow, and both had printed on them the words "Hopedale Penny Post." When carrying the mail I also carried a supply of these stamps in a pen-box in my bag, and if the receiver of a letter had no little stamp to give in return, he usually tendered a silver three-cent piece, and I gave him a stamp. On the outgoing mail the Hopedale stamp was affixed to the middle of the back of the envelope.

There were only fourteen or fifteen houses on my route then, and the Hopedale Home School received the greater number of letters. The best remembered newspapers that came in the mail were the New York *Tribune*, the *Liberator*, Worcester *Spy*, and Woonsocket *Patriot*.

The Post Office

As Hopedale grew the Post Office was transferred to the grocery store, first to the house where I now reside, when Mr. Ansel Harlow was storekeeper and postmaster. I can show you where the hole was cut in my front door to receive the mail. After the Home School was closed and the schoolhouse was altered into a dwelling house, Mr. Hiram Gibson had a grocery store there, and filled both positions. That was in the first house north of the Town House.

I think the little stamp was used until Hopedale had a regular United States Post Office. These stamps have now become objects of interest to stamp collectors. One has recently been sold by a Hopedale lady for five dollars, and had it been a perfect stamp it would have brought her more money.

Sometimes I carried other letters than those that came in "Uncle Sam's" mail-bag. There lived in Hopedale, in a little house at the corner of Union and Dutcher Streets, although Dutcher Street was not there then, four unmarried sisters named Julia, Nancy, Cynthia, and Mary Ann Hayward. Now Mary Ann, albeit the youngest, so much desired to be married that she advertised for a husband in some paper. I think it was the *Phrenological Journal*. One morning Mr. Humphrey came to my father's and asked if I would do an errand for a man who was stopping at his house. I gladly consented, and upon going to the gentleman, received a letter which I was requested to carry to Mary Ann Hayward and wait for a reply. I distinctly remember what excitement prevailed among the sisters and how Mary Ann hastened to pen the answer. This I duly carried to the waiting gentleman and O, what bliss!! I received a bright new ten-cent piece for my trouble.

The man proved to be Justin Soule, who had answered Mary Ann's advertisement. Soon after they were married and, as far as I know, lived happily ever after.

Hopedale, Massachusetts

Anti-Slavery and Other Visitors to the Community

Anna Thwing Field

In the early days of the Community many persons were interested in its establishment; and reformers with varied causes came to present their "isms" and secure a following. It was their custom to receive all who came courteously, to give a patient, candid hearing to whatever cause or progressive idea they advocated, provided always that Mr. Ballou should question, review and confute the whole matter, not only at the time presented, but when discussed for approval or rejection. No hotel received the strangers,–they were entertained at private houses and treated as guests. Mr. Eben Draper's home was oftenest their headquarters. Many were honest, earnest men, but some were cranks. Well I remember the long, long sessions when the various subjects were discussed and the excitement when the adherents and opponents parried questions and answers, till flushed faces and angry gestures followed.

Theodore Parker brought here his then radical ideas of the Bible and Jesus. Samuel J. May and his brother were interested in prison reform and wished substantial aid. Henry Wright came to advocate "free love," and living with your "affinity," kindred topics, but met with a chilling reception, and although he was allowed "free speech," was politely "frozen out." Advocates of frugality in diet were numerous and experiments were tried to reduce the cost of living to the lowest figures without impairing the health. Here came Graham. I well remember the trouble my aunt took sending to Boston to procure graham flour for his cooking, though at supper he astonished her by declining the graham bread and choosing white biscuit, saying he had plenty of graham bread at home. "Consistency, thou art a jewel." Animal magnetism and clairvoyance were presented and their exponents gave many exhibitions at my own home, as did also the spiritual mediums, when the rappings, writing, and tipping of tables were investigated. Two mediums of note dwelt in Hopedale, Fannie Davis Smith and Cora Scott Hatch Tappan.

Reform extended to dress and many women became wearers of the Bloomer costume, a short skirt reaching to the knees with long trousers like the dress. The abbreviated skirts were convenient about the house, but some wore them abroad, made from silk or broadcloth, and were victims of ridicule and amusement in the neighboring towns. Many women gave up their simple earrings, bracelets, etc., feeling it wrong to wear jewelry when so many lacked the comforts of life; knowing also that "a meek and lowly spirit is the greatest ornament."

The Shakers, Quakers and other religious organizations sent representatives to promulgate their peculiar ideals. Peace and temperance advocates were welcome and received prompt endorsement. Edwin Thompson from England was one.

Perhaps the people who interested me most were the abolitionists, for as a child, nothing so stirred my temper or caused my tears to flow, as the wrongs and sorrows of the colored people. Boston was agitating the subject at Faneuil

Hall and in the *Liberator*. Grove meetings were held at South Framingham, and annually in August, in a small pine grove near where the High School building now is, Hopedale had an Anti-Slavery meeting. I recall many earnest men and women who spoke from that platform. There came Parker Pillsbury, the dark-skinned, dark-haired, scowling man, who stormed across the stage, shook his clenched fists and said things that scared one; ably seconded by Charles Burleigh, who wore his hair and beard long, having vowed he never would cut them till the slave was free. William Lloyd Garrison, always in earnest but more moderate in voice and wiser in counsel, was always present, and usually Wendell Phillips with his gentlemanly, polished ways and scholarly oratory.

Among the women speakers were Lucy Stone Blackwell, Abby Kelley Foster and Anna Dickinson. Mrs. Foster was a sister of Grandmother Earl who lived where Mrs. Sornborger now lives. Stephen Foster and his wife were from Worcester and were always friends of the slave. Frederick Douglass, a colored man who was an escaped slave, was an interesting speaker. The weightier matters discussed were advocated in the *Practical Christian*, the newspaper published by the Community, but I was too young to appreciate the ideas that were advanced, that were afterwards the occasion of national dissension and civil war. I was more interested when a man arose on the platform and showed branded in the palm of his uplifted hand the letters S.S. He had labored among the slaves to aid them to escape from slavery and as a punishment was burned S.S. for Slave Stealer. He afterwards married Dr. Emily Gay's sister and lived in Hopedale.

I well remember the black, black man of large stature who was called Henry Box Brown. He was a slave and had come all the way from the South, sent by friends in a dry goods box with holes in the cover, and labeled, "This side up. With care," and shipped, if I remember rightly, to Isaac T. Hopper, New York. Here, too, came Ellen Crafts and her husband, who were of special interest. Ellen was short, slender and light skinned, he was tall and perfectly black. He was a cabinet maker and she a lady's maid and were married as all slaves were, without clergy, no legal marriage. They escaped from slavery, she disguised as a young gentleman and he as her servant. Neither could read or write, so she made a sore on her right hand, bound it up and started North to consult a physician. They came to Charleston on a steamer, then took a carriage for the best hotel, William, anxious for his master's health, securing the best room and service and sleeping on a mat outside his master's door. Every passenger accompanied by a colored servant was obliged to sign a paper declaring that the servant was his slave before they could leave the state, and Ellen asked a gentleman to sign for her as her hand was disabled and he politely complied. Her invalidism increased and that helped them on. They were met in Philadelphia and passed on to Boston, and married by Theodore Parker and then sent to England. After the Civil War they lived in Georgia and worked for the colored people.

Many escaped slaves lived in the families of Hopedale. My father had a colored man called John who did some work about the place, but never went alone from the house. At night he was there, in the morning gone. I was too young to be entrusted with important secrets. In the opposite house a man, woman and two children, all black, dwelt one winter in the cellar kitchen and one summer in the attic. The oldest girl went to school and learned to read and write.

Another neighbor had as a guest Lizzie Hall, a handsome mulatto young woman with a history somewhat like Eliza of *Uncle Tom's Cabin*, though Lizzie Hall was her master's daughter. She stayed till after her little child was born; then she too, had gone away. Several others there were who lived among us for weeks or months. They were fed, clothed, and sheltered. We knew them and saw them moving in and out, one day here, the next, gone. Sometimes we heard they had reached Worcester, Boston, New York, or the Mecca of their wanderings, Canada.

There can be no doubt that the early inhabitants of Hopedale were earnest and conscientious in their devotion to convictions of duty, whatever its cost and penalties.

Milford, Massachusetts

Recollections of Hopedale

Ida D. Smith

Early in the Community Days a Council was formed, called the Council of Religious Conciliation and Justice. To this Council many of the affairs of the Community were referred for settlement. Complaints being made of the behavior of the children and youth connected with the public schools, it was voted that the president of the council should visit the school and reprove the scholars for rude, boisterous and other improper conduct; later a committee was chosen who drew up a statement of what was expected of the youth and aliens residing in the Community Domain, and these rules, after being subjected to the board of education and approved by them, were printed and posted in every tenement, and in all those places where it would prove useful. The hearty cooperation of parents and those who had charge of children was asked. This method proved successful in a measure.

From their Journal we read that on the 26th of July, 1847, the trustees of the Community agreed that Henry Lillie should occupy the "Old House," so called; except the tenement occupied by William Rich, and the south room, which was to be used as an office by the trustees; at the rate of thirty five dollars per year, to be paid quarterly; also that he should have all the milk from the town farm, and furnish the same to individuals at one half cent per quart in advance. Mr. Lillie agreed to take boarders at the rate of one dollar and seventy five cents per week for men, and one dollar and twenty-five cents for women. We also learn that in those early days the sum of twenty-five dollars was allowed each adult person yearly for clothing, and fifteen dollars for children; and each member was allowed to enjoy a ride of fifty miles during the year.

From this Council a Sponsorial Committee was formed whose duty it was to become personally acquainted with the character and sentiments of those desiring to become members, that those thus desiring might have a correct idea of the real burdens and responsibilities. These applicants were to be placed on probation, to receive, while they remained probationers, such treatment for their faults as they would if members in full fellowship. "For it is not the highest Christianity for any one to be knowing to faults and practices in Probationers which are inconsistent with the principles of the Community, without taking some measure to have them corrected. And especially so, when they are brought forward as things which should cause their rejection."

When persons desired to become members the examinations were carefully conducted and if it was found that they were not fully acquainted with the principles but still wished to become co-workers, they were given time for consideration of them.

The meetings of the Council, for the most part, at the homes of the members, were opened by prayer, either vocal or silent, and they often lasted many hours. Intemperance was not tolerated. At one meeting of the Council a lady presented a charge against her husband for exceedingly intemperate habits, and in consequence of his outrageous conduct, and continued threats, she had come to the conclusion that if he staid in the family it must be as a boarder, not as a husband and father. The Council voted that they did not approve of his remaining in the Community, longer, in any capacity. However, later on, the Council called a meeting to consider a written promise from the man to abstain from the use of all intoxicating beverages for the future, and to acquiesce in all the rules and regulations of the Community if allowed to remain in the Domain. Brother Ballou offered to be responsible for his good conduct, and the Council consented to his further residence.

There was but one principal street; where Adin and Dutcher streets are, were dense woods, and where this church stands were rocks and bushes, where we as children played, and picked berries. I remember the clearing of the land and of the Church being built, which a few years ago was torn down that this Memorial Church might be built.

No dogs were allowed in town. On one occasion a family who owned a dog moved here, and so incensed were the people that the owners when told that they must either get rid of the dog or move. The family moved out of town.

Card playing was not countenanced, and, if indulged in, it was in secret. No tobacco was sold, and tea and coffee were to be used sparingly.

The houses were few and far between, very simple in architecture; in many houses the chimneys went only as far as the floor, seldom into the cellar.

The exterior of the houses was made attractive with running vines and had flower gardens around them, the work being done mostly by women clad in bloomers. It was no unusual sight to see women, thus garbed, with wheelbarrow, rake and shovel, at work.

The clothes of the men and women were of the simplest, but always neat and clean. Men wore overalls, and the women, calico dresses, aprons and sunbonnets to church. Flowers in their bonnets were forbidden. When Alonzo Cook brought his bride, who was a schoolteacher from Blackstone, to church, and she wore a silk dress and a bonnet much bedecked with flowers, it was said that they feared Alonzo had married a very extravagant woman. At one time twenty-five women, all clad in bloomers, went in a barge to Worcester, to attend a Women's Rights Convention. They attracted so much attention that the police were called upon to protect them.

Great care was taken with the children – in fact everything was done to promote their happiness. The schools were of the best, so the children were educated in the most approved manner. Their physical education commenced in a common nursery, into which they were received with the consent of their parents, then promoted to higher grades.

Margaret Fish had a Sewing Class and at one of the sales we realized a little over two dollars, this money being used to buy shoes for the poor children of Milford.

The custom of observing the birthdays of members, both old and young, was said to be truly affecting, profitable and refreshing. Original songs were sung, and appropriate remarks were always made by members.

A man by the name of Edmund Soward, being interested in the Hopedale Community, came here to live. He was very much interested in the education and social welfare of the young. In his will he left most of his property to the Community, in trust, to be expended in the culture and comfort of the children of Hopedale. On one ever to be remembered. occasion, Reverend W. S. Heywood told the younger school children that on the following Saturday we were to go to Boston to see the trained seals and mice, the money to defray the expenses to be taken from the Soward Fund. Great excitement prevailed. One little girl asked her mother what she should wear for a wrap, and when told she could wear her sister's cape, she replied, "Why, everybody will know it is my sister's, because she wore it last spring when she went to Boston." We took our dinners and ate them on Boston Common.

We were brought up very strictly; children were supposed to be in the house, if not in bed, by nine o'clock at night.

We were taught obedience in all things. One Fourth of July there was to be an unusual celebration in Milford; Hopedale being then part of Milford, the school children were to march through the streets, the band to play, the children to sing patriotic songs and carry flags. Now this was contrary to the Non-Resistance principles of the Community, so when our parents were interviewed we were not allowed to join in the exercises.

A general kindly feeling existed among the members of the Community. It was like one large family.

As one walks through the streets of Hopedale, under the forest trees transplanted to adorn the village street and to stand as sentinels through the coming years, he cannot help but feel that God has blessed the hands of those early workers.

Hopedale, Massachusetts

Reminiscences of the "Home School" and the Village

Imogene Mascroft

Is it possible that fifty years have rolled their slow course along since my father deposited me and my small trunk at the front door of the Home School, where I spent the most of two happy years, a half century behind us? Surely that suggests spectacles, gray hair, corpulence, wrinkles, and rheumatism. Memory also begins to lag. Mine, at least, is not so prompt at my bidding as she was a score of years ago, but many of the pleasant memories of those years in Hopedale are safely stowed away never to be forgotten.

Reminiscences of the Home School would seem no hopeless task, but interesting chronicles of the village is another matter, for if my memory serves me right, we were but little acquainted, either with the village or its people. To be sure our Gospel teachings on Sundays we obtained at the little school house at the upper end of the village about opposite the large shop, now made over into a dwelling house. Here we went in the morning for Sunday School, and again in the afternoon for Church Services. Usually Mr. Ballou occupied the teacher's desk which served for the pulpit, exchanging frequently with Mr. Heywood.

I also remember the Saturday night dancing parties which were held in the second story of one of the shops. I know we went up a rickety stairway into a large, unoccupied room, which served as a sort of hall, in an old red building. Machinery of various kinds occupied the lower floor, but we had great fun dancing till, I believe, about half past nine, when an intermission or lull in the music (I think it was a violin and accordion) would be the favorable opportunity that Mr. Lowell Heywood would take, to request the Home School scholars to go home, and we would go, feeling very much abused.

The Main Street of the village is changed almost beyond recognition. Indeed, one can hardly help feeling as forlorn as did Rip Van Winkle in returning to his old home, so much that was familiar is gone. The store of H. L. Patrick, on the Milford road, was not then built. Speaking of that store reminds me of the early ambition of the proprietor. A favorite morning exercise at the opening of school was to express in a few words our dreams of future greatness and what large place in life we hoped to fill. Henry's taste for mercantile pursuits had probably not developed, for he then expected to become a circus rider.

The old school house and the boarding house near it look fairly natural, but I miss the pleasant home of the Humphreys with its garden of flowers, especially the roses; also the little cottage homes of Mary Reed and Dr. Emily Gay, who, by the way, at that time, was a familiar figure on the street, dressed in her bloomer costume, whose only justification was its convenience, carrying her little medicine chest, hurrying along with her swinging arms and gait, doubtless reaching her patient's side in good time, even if a runabout had not been heard of.

I also remember well Harriet N. Green Butts and her husband, although the latter is hardly anything but a myth in my mind.

The beautiful church of today, I think, must occupy about the same site of one built about 1860. The most delightful association with that place was our happy reunion in 1867, a day long to be remembered by all who were privileged to be present.

An old house that I miss in my frequent visits to Hopedale is one in some way connected with the old Community, in my day occupied by a family by the name of Moore. It has probably gone the way of many other old landmarks and is no more. One can afford to spare much in exchange for the fine Library and Town Hall, and numerous other buildings that take their places.

The side streets leading from Main, on which have been built so many beautiful residences, were not even laid out. The usual way of reaching Milford was over the hill from the Mendon road. An old stage coach went back and forth as a public conveyance once or twice a day, but we Home School scholars usually annihilated the distance by walking; that is, when we could get permission, which wasn't often. The old stage coach and the tired horses that dragged it over the hill are no more – peace to their ashes! In their stead, as if by magic, shining rails traverse the quiet streets, over which speed half hourly trolley cars, which in our day were not even dreamed of. But I must not let my pen stray away into the past save to assure you that were I to allow it full license you would weary of its wanderings.

Changes, many and strange, have come to all of us, as well as the village, since we went out from the protection of the dear old Home School, and experience has taught us many a lesson, since we recited so glibly in yonder recitation room. I remember my zeal and love for Hopedale was so great, that when I said, "Goodbye," I fully intended that all my sons and daughters should be sent here to be fitted after the most approved manner for higher posts of influence and usefulness. Alas, for my dreams! The juveniles did not materialize, and the Home School is no more. That it once existed, and I was permitted to belong to it; and for the friendships formed there, which add much pleasure to the waning years; these are events in my life; for which I am ever entirely thankful.

Uxbridge, Massachusetts

The Burglary

Susan Thwing Whitney

In the early Hopedale days, when a stranger came to the place, he was directed to Mr. William Humphrey's for food and lodging. The house occupied by Mr. and Mrs. Humphrey stood just where West Hope Street is, and was torn down when that street and the bridge were built.

One night Miss Lizzie Humphrey was awakened by strange and unusual noises. After satisfying herself that someone was prowling around the house, she partially dressed, went down stairs and told her parents what she had heard. They arose and upon looking round found the dining-room silver packed in a bag, and the feet of a man were protruding from under the end of the long, haircloth sofa in the parlor.

Lizzie hastened to arouse the neighbors. Mr. Ballou, Mr. Eben Draper, Mr. Thwing and Arthur Clark, a boarder at Mr. Thwing's, were summoned, and they called some others.

Here was a dilemma which had not previously confronted the people of Hopedale.

There was no policeman here then, no lock-up, and the non-resistant principles of the people kept them from using violence in any form, but something must be done, and that quickly.

The parlor extended across the entire front of the house and had two doors, one of which opened into the front hall, and the other into the dining room. At each of these doors, a man was stationed and if the prisoner tried to escape, they were to call the other men who were in consultation.

Many were the questions which arose. Who was he? Was he armed? Would he come from his hiding-place if ordered to do so, and what should they do with him when they had him? At last it was decided that all should enter the parlor, and four men should lift the sofa away from the burglar, while the others should capture him if he tried to escape.

Imagine the procession headed by one man carrying an old-fashioned oil-lamp. Cautiously they advanced, lifted the sofa, and lo, they beheld a poor, half-witted fellow, whom the Humphreys had recently fed, doctored and otherwise befriended.

He sat up and surveyed the company. When questioned as to why he was there and in that condition, he answered that he had no home and could find nothing to do, and he thought if he came there and stole something, the Humphreys would send him to some place where he would, at least, have enough to eat. After stopping with them for a time that is just what they did do.

Later, when some one asked Mrs. Humphrey if she didn't feel real provoked with him for returning all their kindness in that way, she, the dear, kind-hearted woman, replied, "Why, no; I felt as if I wanted to take him right in my arms."

Hopedale, Massachusetts

Our Community School and its Teacher

Ellen M. Patrick

Old Hopedale has passed, but not its influence. This new demand for social justice, with the Socialist vision of the future, is the same Community dream given a world-wide sweep. Who can trace the subtle influence linking the past and present, or measure the effect, "greatening as it journeys on," of the consecration, prayers, and self-sacrificing devotion to the ideals of brotherhood of the founders of Hopedale?

Let me quote: "First, a thought, a wish, then a faith; next, a struggle; at last, a fact. So have entered into human life and history some of its profoundest truths."

But Hopedale still lives in a small and lessening number of those who shared its life and were molded by it. We always carry our ancestors about with us; and there are early influences from which we never escape, which, indeed, may determine our lives. Some of us would not have been ourselves as we know our aptitudes and feelings, our point of view, without Hopedale and all it stood for.

As I look back, I see many helpers of the spirit who made what might seem plain and prosaic village life beautiful in its round and noble in its outlook, but I name today only the one who most of all left a permanent impress on the minds and hearts of the Hopedale youth, our dear Miss

Abbie, when first I knew her; after her marriage, Mrs. Abbie, our devoted and beloved teacher and friend.

The school was nominally under the supervision of the committee of the town of Milford, and I recall that we were proud to have these weighty visitants. Who could forget ponderous Priest Woodbury? We always knew they came to praise; for was not ours a model school?

Our Mrs. Abbie was a Normal graduate, handsome and loving, with insight, originality and personal power, the ideal teacher. She anticipated so-called modern methods. We were proud of the really remarkable maps with meridians and parallels that we used to put on the board from memory. I hope I am not, after the fashion of aged people, seeing double through the dim vista of years, but those maps are before me away back in the fifties, and the old thrill of satisfaction. But we stood on the pinnacle of pride when following our teacher in numerical combinations as she flashed them off with amazing rapidity. What a sense of power this splendid training gave us! Possibly a real enlargement of life.

We were given instruction in drawing. Gilbert Thompson, whose affection for the old place and friends was strong to the last, and who had hoped to share in these memories, was able to take up the work of a topographical engineer, without farther preparation, and to become, finally, a leading topographer; and Lizzie Humphrey, our real artist, received here her first preparation for the career in which she won distinction. Dear Lizzie, loveliest of girls, and always our Queen of the May.

Our school was known among reformers. A son of Garrison and of Samuel May were sent to Hopedale to attend it. Reverend William Fish, learned in languages and universities, once said that Mrs. Abbie was, he believed, the best teacher he ever had; which happily bears out his tribute as a small boy, when he wished, in a composition letter, that he might live to be a hundred and go to school to Mrs. Abbie every day of his life.

I find that our memory of the past is in flash-light pictures. Here is one of the brightest. Our schoolroom was our Sunday Chapel, and I can see her yet, our Miss Abbie, even to the dainty silk she wore, on the bright Sunday morning, standing before us as she became our Mrs. Abbie. We knew it was joy for her, and we, too, were glad. And, now, as we all go on together in the "lengthening shadows" of life's afternoon, we feel the tenderest sympathy for her loss and loneliness – but we are glad that she is with us still, our dear friend and helper in the spirit.

Hopedale, Massachusetts

Christmas in the Old Days

Frank J. Dutcher

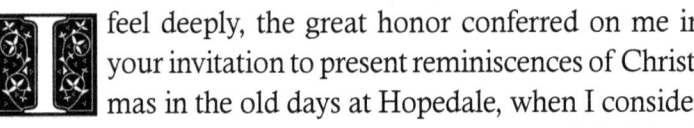feel deeply, the great honor conferred on me in your invitation to present reminiscences of Christmas in the old days at Hopedale, when I consider how many there are present who are better qualified, both by age and experience, to make this contribution to your program.

Some five or six years ago, when serving as Chairman of the Christmas Committee, it occurred to me that a little preface to the regular exercises might be of interest, as so few who now attend the afternoon entertainment had any idea of what led up to the present arrangement. I made a few notes, but unfortunately, between moving and other incidents due to the lapse of time, they were not preserved, and I am therefore obliged to make a fresh start.

In these days of Christmas trees, public and private, in all religious denominations, it is difficult to realize that the evolution of the Christmas tree in this country covers comparatively few years; and that the little village of Hopedale was one of the pioneers in this line, some sixty years ago.

It is desirable at the outset to remember that the Hopedale environment at that time was quite different. Hopedale was a village of 200 to 300 people, in the town of Milford.

Our highways included the present Main Street running from Mendon to Milford past Mr. O. B. Young's, with Freedom Street at the northerly limit as the only other road to Milford. Freedom Street at that time went to Mendon up the steep hill past the "Salt-Box" place, now occupied by the Dillon family. Hopedale Street connected the roads through the center of the place. Dutcher Street, then called High Street, only existed in the imagination, with the exception of the short section connecting Social and Union streets. The only road to the cemetery was a rough cart path through a succession of pastures; and in case of a funeral, it was necessary to pass through several pairs of bars. There were no good sidewalks.

The entire village did not include over fifty houses, nearly all for one family each. There were only two houses west of the river, these being the one at the end of the pond, now occupied by Mr. Willard, and the Soward house directly back of it. The only public building was the Chapel. This is the building now occupied by Mr. Gilbert Arnold and adjoining the School grounds. This Chapel was used for all gatherings, religious or secular, and on week days was occupied by the Public School. It had a small bell tower at the end next the street and was equipped with a clock made by a local artist, Mr. Almon Thwing. The bell was used for both School and Church.

With this small isolated community, affairs of Church and State were closely identified. Up to 1856 all families, or at least one of the heads, belonged to the Community, and thus all church services and festivals were of general interest.

My first Christmas at Hopedale was in the year 1856, and to obtain earlier data I have looked over the file of the

Practical Christian, a semi-weekly paper edited by Mr. Ballou and published from 1840 to 1860. Unfortunately the early volumes were devoted more to controversial and other matters than to local news, and the first mention of the local Christmas exercises at length, is in what was called the "Youths' Department," edited by Mrs. Margaret E. Fish, in the January 14th issue of 1854.

The following extracts are from three long columns of special report:

> ### CHRISTMAS FESTIVAL
>
> The people of Hopedale had a Christmas festival on Saturday, Dec. 24th, ult., commencing at 2:30 P. M. The exercises commenced by singing an original hymn, composed by Joseph Bailey. A prayer was then offered by Wm. H. Fish, which was succeeded by a welcome spoken by Eddie Hewitt, aged about 11, after which we listened to a song from the infant class, "Let Us Love One Another."

An address was then delivered by Adin Ballou. (I omit the summary of the address.)

> The address was followed by a song from the little children commencing, "I want to be an angel." We next listened to a declamation from Ida Albee, and another by Eben Bancroft, little children about 6 years of age. Then Willie Fish and Willie Draper spoke the Dialogue between William Penn and King Charles. Two declamations followed, one by Ellen Walker, aged about 9, another by Amanda Albee, "The Best Use of a Penny."
>
> Then came some thrilling music performed by Willie Draper on the seraphine, Lyman Allen on the flute and W. W. Cook on the violin. A piece was then spoken by Frances Draper, aged about 6, entitled, "Is It Sunday?" Little Susan Thwing then spoke a piece of poetry illustrating the Mother's Love. Next came a piece spoken by Joseph Harlow aged

about 12, which was followed by a dialogue by three little children, Asa Inman, Eben Bancroft and Susan Thwing, showing the unhappiness arising from selfishness.

"The Three Prayers" was then spoken by Lizzie Wentworth, about 9 years of age; a declamation followed from Asa Inman, 5 or 6 years of age. Then we had a fairy song, which the writer of this sketch was not ethereal enough to understand.

"Take the spade of Perseverance,
Dig the field of Progress wide"

was then spoken by Lizzie Humphrey, about 13 years of age.

The reporter goes on with an additional array of single declamations by Emily Sutcliff, Hattie Walker, Anne Munyan, Elisha Davis, Allen Price, Lucy Lillie and others. Dialogues of two, four and six characters each are interspersed with extracts and descriptions.

We then had some conundrums which were got up for the occasion by Joseph Bailey, and were in the form of a dialogue, and spoken by four young persons. This excited some mirth which seemed to be relished ... The exercises were closed by a song, "Good Night."

Midway in the program "came a simple repast of bread and butter, plain cake, and popped corn."

About an hour before the speaking closed, the curtains which had through the afternoon concealed the Christmas Tree, were drawn aside, and we were permitted to behold the pliant branches of the hemlock, drooping under a load of rich presents, whose varied colors were pleasing to the eye. At seven o'clock in the evening the distribution of presents commenced. There were four or five persons actively engaged in taking the presents from the tree and reading the names of those for whom the presents were hung. After each article was announced, and the name of the person that was to possess it, it was put into the hand of some little girl to carry to the place where the person was seated.

After the establishment of the Home School under the management of Mr. and Mrs. Wm. S. Heywood, in 1856, another feature was added, namely a dramatic number. The program, as I remember it, included single pieces and short dialogues, to include all the village children, prayer and address by the available minister; songs by the children being sandwiched in at intervals. Many of the people carried their suppers, eating them at intermission between the afternoon and evening parts of the entertainment. At seven o'clock or thereabouts came the tree, followed by a play or musical number. "Neighbor Jackwood" is one play that I recall. Another year we had the Cantata of Esther.

Some of those present will remember the curtains, green at the center and alternate breadths of blue and reddish brown at the sides. The church building erected in 1860 was provided with the same curtains, refitted, and the center curtains pieced out. It was a job requiring the greatest skill to rig up these curtains for Christmas. During the balance of the year they were stored in the attic.

The fact that it was too late for the children when the tree was not shown until evening, led to a change in the program. For quite a number of years we commenced in the afternoon at one-thirty or thereabouts. The exercises included an anthem by the choir, prayer and address by the minister, dialogues, songs and recitations by the children, usually with a piece introducing the tree. The presents were distributed in the afternoon and it was often five o'clock by the time we adjourned. In the evening there was a dramatic entertainment by local talent, the parts being taken in most cases by the young people.

The Christmas committee was usually chosen the Sunday before Thanksgiving. The Chairman was selected largely for his ability to pay the expenses.

When the tree was at the Chapel, presents were left at the home of Mr. and Mrs. E. D. Draper and taken from there to the Chapel and hung Christmas forenoon. When we moved to the Church, this arrangement was changed, and presents were taken by the committee the afternoon and evening before at the Church, the committee putting as many as practicable on the tree in the evening. Someone prepared for emergencies always remained in the Church over night.

One of the most effective plays ever put on was "The Chimney Corner." The stage setting was very realistic, showing an old-time room with the mantel and corner cupboard from the old house then recently torn down. Mr. Wm. H. Humphrey and myself worked nearly the entire time between the closing of the afternoon entertainment until time to open in the evening in erecting this material for the stage. That evening our local orchestra furnished the music, as we did in several other cases.

Hopedale, Massachusetts

Childhood Days in the Hopedale Community, and Other Recollections

Nellie T. Gifford

rom the many recollections of long ago, those I am giving are mostly of childhood days in Hopedale Community, where my father's family came Nov. 1853, our first home being in an old-fashioned red house belonging to Newton Daniels, on the site of which, I think, now stands Governor Draper's barn. A few months later we moved into the so-called "Water Cure" house, which was our home for many years.

My school experience in Hopedale began in the building now occupied by Mr. Arnold, then half its size, later enlarged. It also served as church, and for all public meetings, and was heated in winter by a small box stove. A little room at one side of the entrance, used for storage purposes, was also the children's Sunday School Library, books being kept on shelves in a wooden closet. The adults' library, on the other side, was more pretentious, having a large bookcase with glass doors.

In the basement was the Community variety store, kept by Mr. Munyan, afterward by Mr. Swazey. Mrs. Abbie Heywood, (we called her "Mrs. Abbie") was my first teacher, Mrs. Mulliken the second, for both of whom I have pleasant memories. Across the pond lived Mr. Soward, who taught us writing. His cousin and housekeeper, Aunty Burton, was a quaint, kindly woman, with a badly disfigured face, caustic in criticism, but a favorite with all. The schoolhouse was the scene of many happy festivals, that at Christmas being an especially joyous one for children, some taking part in the exercises and all sure of a gift from the tree.

My first impression at Church was vividly remembered, it seemed so queer to see dignified women appear in bloomer dresses, some made with quite snug fitting "pants," others full and gathered at the ankle, with a narrow frill falling over the shoe. In summer some ladies wore to church, sunbonnets – quite a contrast to the present style of head covering.

Hopedale was a music loving community. A trio, Edward Stimpson, George Young, and my brother Charles, often gave vocal selections, Origen Young accompanying on a melodeon. Joshua Hutchinson, one of the famous family of singers, gave several concerts, and one winter conducted a singing school in the place. For a time there was no instrumental music at church service, but later a melodeon was used, Amanda Albee, a sister of Mrs. Ida Smith, playing the hymns. At the dedication of the large Community Barn (afterward converted into a tannery) children assisted with declamation and songs; two verses of one written by a village poet, I recall:

> The rose when crushed gives back perfume,
> To blows, rich fragrance follows soon;
> Fair rose, thou lovely Christian flower,
> We'd be like thee, in trial's hour.

> Then why should we not love the flowers
> That grow about this Dale of ours,
> Sweet tokens they will ever prove
> Of our dear Father's bounteous love.

Children had many amusements, simple but enjoyable, among them occasional rides in the large and only boat on the pond; skating and coasting in winter; berrying and picnics in summer; hanging May baskets all through the month; and hunting wild flowers in the fields and sprout land woods growing on part of what is now Dutcher Street.

After a time dancing was allowed for adults and children, Mr. Ballou approving, as to quote his words, "Innocent recreation in due season accords with true Religion." The dance hall was in the upper part of the Dutcher shop; hours for dancing from 6 to 9.30 P. M. John Moore, a fine clarinetist, and Mr. Cross of Milford, violinist, furnished music; Mr. Cross being also teacher and prompter. Square and Contra dances, only, were allowed, masculine arms encircling feminine waists, as in polka and waltz, being considered detrimental by some of the elders.

I well remember the shock to the Community caused by the death, in a railroad accident, of Dr. Butler Wilmarth, and not long after, the drowning, in a pool in front of the Samuel Walker estate, of a son of Aunty Johnson, a colored woman whom many will remember. In those early days the dead were taken to the cemetery in a large wagon, friends following on foot.

The Community was strongly Anti-Slavery in sentiment, and the celebrations of Emancipation in the West Indies, held in "Nelson's Grove," were enthusiastic events, enjoyed too by the children. Some noted speakers would be present, among them Garrison, Phillips, Abby Kelley Foster, Charles Burleigh, whose features so strongly resembled pictures of Christ, and Sojourner Truth, once a slave, a powerful, if not cultured, advocate of freedom for those of her race in bondage. She was a large, very black woman, very witty;

and an inveterate smoker. The late Theodore Tilton once asked her how she expected "to enter Heaven with a tobacco scented breath." Her reply was, "When I die and go to Heaven, I 'spect to leave my bref behind me." The "Man with the Branded Hand" was at one time a resident of Hopedale. He was called so, as in aiding slaves to escape, he was caught by owners, and the letters S. S. (Slave Stealer) burned in his hand.

In the olden days, no dogs were allowed in the village; no liquor or tobacco sold; drunkards rarely seen; tramps unknown; the front doors of houses being left open summer nights, with no fear of anything but cool breezes entering.

I think no one dreamed then what a vast increase in manufacturing was to come! The shop by the pond was a small affair, the making of nipper blocks and hatchets, two of the industries carried on in it. My father had a small room for his drafting and pattern making. A wooden building opposite the Dutcher shop contained the counting room, tin, and carpenter shops; a room in which at one time Pliny Southwick kept shoes for sale; and a room where two girls set temple teeth. My brother carried on a bindery in a part, now demolished, of the house at the corner of Union and Dutcher streets. This house was built by an Englishman, who in telling of his plans for it, said he was going to "'ave 'hells' on it." Miss Bailey now lives in one of the "hells."

It was not strange that residents should differ in opinion. Some were vegetarians, regarding the use of meat as a food, wrong, and at one time the Lyceum was the scene of heated arguments between those who favored and those who opposed its use. One family advocated such an extremely plain diet, that it was rumored theirs consisted chiefly of "peat and molasses."

Preparing ground for the new Church was done by the Industrial Army, composed of men of the village. There was rejoicing when the Church was finished and dedicated.

Among the villagers were some odd characters; one old resident, Mr. Bowers, was quite original in his remarks. He believed in early rising, and used to say, "Folks lie abed so late now, the next generation won't get up at all."

Of the "Old House" and its inmates, I have pleasant recollections, and it seems as if no water has ever tasted as good as that drawn from the depths of the "Old Home" well.

I remember the great crop of peaches, one fall, and the extreme cold of the following winter which killed all the trees that bore them. Where once nearly every garden had its peach trees, few are now to be seen.

One prominent event in Hopedale history occurred when Mr. Morgan Bloom, who had previously been connected with the Five Points Mission in New York City, opened a Home School for boarding and day pupils, irrespective of color; a school later conducted for several years by Mr. and Mrs. William S. Heywood.

The Civil War wrought a great change in Hopedale. Excitement ran high, and with some, the Non-Resistant principles were overcome by the "Spirit of '76." The Post Office was at that time a room in the house now occupied by Mrs. Susan Whitney, and at mail time was filled with a crowd eager for the New York *Tribune*, with its details of the killed and wounded in engagements. The battlefield, "Andersonville Prison Pen," and disease claimed as victims several who enlisted from Hopedale, and the peaceful life of the village was over for a time.

Since then Hopedale has become a flourishing town; many of the old residents have passed away, and old landmarks are fast disappearing; but as advancing years bring more vividly memories of the past with its joys and sorrows, I realize that some of the happiest hours of my life were those spent in "Old Community Days."

Fitchburg, Massachusetts

Hopedale Community, Founded in 1841: Its Origin and Early History

Abbie Ballou Heywood

Should the article here presented to you savor somewhat of the egotistical, please to understand the fact, that it may be and probably is true that no one now in the earth life knows personally, now, as much of the origin and earliest history of the Hopedale Community, as does the writer of these reminiscences.

They are written in part at the request of friends who would be better acquainted with its origin, and in part too, to refresh my own memory with its several details.

The time is well remembered when a few friends assembled at my father's house in Mendon, where he was then settled as minister of the Unitarian Society. The subject of Social Reform occupied largely their attention. Charles Fourier, a Frenchman, had been studied, and his principles to some extent adopted, by Robert Dale Owen. Following his theories somewhat, they decided upon a standard which should embody their ideas of a Christian life, calling together those who could subscribe to such a standard, and if practical, found a new social order. Accordingly this Community was started and known as Fraternal Community No. 1, at Mendon, by some thirty individuals from different parts of the state. They were poor in all the resources necessary to

Hopedale Community, Founded in 1841   49

prosecute this great enterprise save faith, zeal, and determination.

They purchased what was called the "Jones Farm," a tract of land lying between Mendon and Milford, alias "The Dale," prefixing the word, "Hope," to its ancient designation, as significant of the great things they hoped for, from an humble, unpropitious beginning. It then contained only two hundred fifty-eight acres and a shabby two-story house, more than one hundred twenty years old, and some outside buildings.

Fourier placed great strength upon the doctrine of Circumstances, as the chief remedial cause of all life's ills. These were tried, but failed to accomplish the result sought. My father did not object to their *modus operandi*, but laid greater stress upon the moral and spiritual element as essential to man's highest development. True to these convictions, two or three families with their dependents moved thither early in the spring of 1842. These were followed by my father's family who together entered upon their untried experiment. True to their pledged cause, and to each other, they were happy in this first step toward an anticipated glorious fruition.

They published to the world their attempt to live "Peace on Earth, Good Will to Men." Daily, letters and friends poured in upon them, too many for their limited means. Most of those who came were ready to accommodate themselves to circumstances, and all the old buildings were speedily overrun with occupants seeking for a restful home, free from the discouragements and disappointments found in individualism. Alas! they little realized that their own imperfections might engulf them in the ruin they sought to escape.

In 1851, the "Old House" in which most of the members had been domiciled, as I have said before, was more than one hundred and twenty years old; their domain consisted of five hundred acres; of twenty-five dwelling houses; three machine shops with water power; facilities for manufacturing; and a small chapel for educational, moral, and spiritual enlightenment. There were then about thirty-four families and in all one hundred and seventy-five persons.

They had many burdens, anxieties, and trials which the true-hearted alone could bear with cheerfulness, and by patient forbearance overcome. Notwithstanding all, its devoted friends now considered it an established institution destined ultimately to exert a glorious influence toward the regeneration of individual and social life.

Previous to this, they had erected a new house, 32 feet by 14 feet above the basement, for a schoolroom, two upper sleeping rooms; and a printing office, where their organ, the *Practical Christian*, was printed every fortnight for twenty years, and continued to proclaim the pure Christian ideals of a ransomed race. It was published from 1840 to 1860. It ended April 1, 1860.

There were four or five preachers who addressed our people and those of surrounding regions on Sunday, and at other times as invited or urged. Regular meetings were held on Sunday, in the Home; a conference meeting for praise and exhortation on Thursday evening.

To maintain discipline in the "Old House" and to keep so many lively boys and girls in order, it was necessary to resort to various expedients. Among these was calling them together to listen to rhymes, which they might learn, perhaps, inculcating their various duties, in and about the house. Some may here be noted in part.

Rhymes

I'll think and. take care how I stamp, stamp, stamp,
When I traverse the rooms, above or below
And never disturb with a wild horse tramp, tramp,
The feelings of those to whom noise is a woe.

I'll think, too, when opening or shutting the door,
To do it so softly and still and unheard,
That no one shall complain of me more
As a heedless, neglectful, wild passage bird.

I'll think of my voice, my coarse, loud, voice,
How it sounds when I scream, or yell, or halloo,
And endeavor to keep it so close and choice,
As never to make any needless ado.

I'll speak in a whisper, or gentle low tone
So kind, and so pleasant, so grateful to hear
That all my superiors and equals shall own
Me, a welcome companion, accepted and dear.

I'll think of my temper, my wayward old will,
So surly and stubborn, so peevish and cross,
That now I must labor to quell all its ills,
And trust in my Savior to purge out the dross.

Blessed work of reform,
O, I'll sing, sing, sing,
As I hie to the task of reform now begun,
And never get weary or dread anything,
Till the great and good work is thoroughly done.

Amusements, combined with the educational, were considered indispensable, and the several evenings of the week were accordingly appropriated to this end. Monday evening was devoted to the young, in general, elevating talks. These were afterwards merged into the Inductive

Communion, so called, which has here before been treated in a comprehensive manner.

Tuesday evening was the night given to the Lyceum, a popular organization in the world at large, when lectures, discussions, and classes came before the assembled people. There were classes in Chemistry, Botany, and Philosophy, examined in a general review. These classes had their stated hours through the week for study and recitation. It may seem somewhat singular that the class in Botany, in the summer, chose to meet at five o'clock in the morning at the "Old House," and then they sallied forth for such rare plants as they might find, returning in an hour, for study and analysis. They were led by some competent teacher in this branch. That the attraction for these morning walks was not always for the study, I leave the hearer to judge. Wednesday eve was given usually to the social claims pertaining to the Association when the various phases were canvassed, always creating an unusual interest.

Dancing among the members generally was abjured, and as a substitute marching was introduced by one of our procurators, similar to the contra dance. A dozen or more couples took the floor, while one of our veterans, skilled on the violin, furnished the music. The room over the shop was utilized for this purpose. Old and young mingled in the entertainment, and the following prophetic Community lines were sung, in which nearly all united. These were composed by one of the original ministers, to whom I shall refer, who was always devising schemes with which to divert and interest the people, and especially the young, with whom he was a favorite. They were not only prophetic, but inspirational.

I copy here the significant lines in part.

Hopedale Community, Founded in 1841

We have come from various quarters,
Both parents, sons, and daughters,
We have come from various quarters
To live a truer life.
And here we stand, joined heart and hand,
And here we hope to win the day,
Oppose who will, oppose who may;
And here we hope to win the day
And live a truer life.

'Twas not the want of affection
For any dear connection,
'Twas not the want of affection,
That brought us to this place.
But 'twas the love of God above
And all our fellow creatures,
Whate'er their hue or features;
And all our fellow creatures
Of all the human race.

We've met with many trials,
Have had some self-denials,
We've met with many trials
In founding here a home.
Yet here we stand, joined heart and hand,
And here we mean to conquer sin,
Our foes without and foes within;
Then Heaven on earth will here begin
For humble souls a home.

Now all our prospects brighten,
Experience doth enlighten,
Small matters do not frighten,
In order we progress.
We labor all, both great and small;
All energies uniting,
Makes labor more inviting,

Activity delighting
Right onward now we press.

In our sequestered dwelling,
All nature's voice impelling,
Kind hearts with love are swelling
For human want and woe.
Our Father's near, we need not fear,
But place our furrow deeply,
And sing our songs more sweetly,
In all good works act meekly
And onward, onward, go.

A part only of these stanzas are inscribed. All present united, singing them with spirit and animation.

The long table with thirty or more guests gave a pleasing variety. After breakfast, the roll was called; each responding to the number of hours they had been employed the previous day.

My father in mentioning the condition of things at this time was much encouraged, saying, "We are unlearning old dispositions, habits, tastes and manners, acquiring new ones, as we trust for the better. Inquirers are coming more and more frequently and we press forward with determined step to the fulfillment of our high mission."

About this time there were many visitors who lectured on various themes. Being amenable as we were, to new ideas, each lecturer readily found a place. The subject of Phrenology was then claiming public attention and the appearance of a man treating this theme, with a "bust" of a finely organized head, was welcomed. He explained in a long poetical dissertation the theories advanced, examined heads, stated their various proclivities, as one after another came forward for predictions. The room was well filled, the attention good, and at an early hour they generally retired; well satisfied with the thought on Phrenology, as expressed by the lecturer.

Strange and crude ideas existed among many, respecting the community finance, in the world outside. For instance, a man of wealth, the husband of a widow with whom I had once boarded, when attending school, called to see and learn what such a peculiar people were like. Walking around to visit the shops, he spoke to me, saying as he did so, and passing me fifty cents, "Do not put this into the Community purse, but in your pocket; buy candy and knickknacks with it when you please. Say nothing to nobody." Of course I took his kindly advice, and the money was placed in a safe repository. A common purse existed in the minds of many, whereas it was a Joint Stock Association.

It was an episode in our circle when a young man appeared, attired in a garb of white, with large books under his arm, and we were elated at the idea that a "Brook Farm" student had come to us to enliven our passing days. He had some cherished ideas, one of which was to summon the boys and girls early in the summer morning, to weed with him in the garden. This was a taking novelty for awhile and was very pleasing, so that fresh recruits were daily added to our number. At length, however, the new wore off and the idea of weeding was relinquished for another morning nap. The young man's white apparel was soon exchanged for an ordinary suit, more appropriate to his duties, and more in accordance with the custom in vogue.

In 1843, one of the original ministers became so dissatisfied, that he sought a home among the Shakers, and soon after sent a thrilling letter to the Secretary, stating that he had found an Elysium. How long he remained with the good people, deponent saith not, but it is to be presumed that he continued to seek the more divine.

Slang and oaths among the members were rare, and I recall none; although what is so common in these days, probably existed to some extent then.

Singing was a prominent amusement and on Friday evenings, we often engaged in Temperance and other secular songs. What a dull entertainment for our young people now, only fascinated with card playing, dancing, and similar amusements! It was not tedious, those days.

Being fond of children, another young girl and I were ordinarily assigned a position in the nursery group, where I managed at times, three or four cradles, while the mothers engaged in household duties. Fortunate was I, when the occupants of the cradles did not all at once demand too much of my attention and left me time for reading.

Each month was held some festive gathering in which, all participated. One of the first was the "Haymakers," when a song was introduced in which the pet names of the horses and the cattle were brought in, as "Nabby," "Dick," and "Trotty," of the horses – I think it was in the days of "King Alcohol," "Buck," etc., of the oxen. These excited some merriment. Other festivals as May and Christmas had a place. The latter, as you know, continues to the present time. This was looked forward to as the gala day of the year. Then appeared our conundrum master with his humorous play upon the names of some of our number, which were acceptable to the company. Gifts were plentiful for old and young. Poets were common with us, and all along they interspersed their poetical effusions. The most gifted of these was Mrs. Abby H. Price who generously served us on festive days, as on the more sad and serious, for nearly ten years, when she sought more congenial surroundings. Others of no ordinary merit might be named did time permit. At one of our May Festivals a very pleasing exercise was presented. Several children marched into the Chapel bearing bouquets of wild flowers, singing as they entered:

> We have been in search of wild flowers
> In Hopedale's glens and shady bowers,
> And gathered each a fair bouquet
> To celebrate this festal day.
>
> And why should we not love the flowers
> That grow about this dale of ours.
> Sweet tokens they will ever prove
> Of our dear Father's precious love.

I omit the remaining excellent stanzas. If any are interested I refer them to p. 182, in the *History of the Hopedale Community*, to be obtained in your Memorial Library. The author of these lines was our kind friend, Reverend D. S. Whitney, and are well worth reading and repeating in song. Henry C. Wright, a great social reformer and peace man, was present, and so much pleased was he with this exercise and others, that he sent an enthusiastic letter to a friend in Europe, and also a western letter describing what he had witnessed.

One of the original ministers, Mr. Stacy, later residing in Milford, whose wife was opposed to Communal life, erected the first dwelling house in the village, on the site now occupied by Mrs. C. M. Day's mansion, on Hopedale Street.

My parents, much worn and weary with their experiences in the Old House, decided to build a home of their own, to live "under their own vine and fig tree," and prosecute their labors for the good of mankind. They accordingly erected a cottage on Peace Street nearby where now stands my father's monument. This was the third house in the village. Their labors were not much diminished, so large a number of visitors was constantly seeking a haven of rest, which they believed Hopedale Community alone could afford. Without money and without price they entertained many such inquirers for several years, still hoping for a blessed fruition of their work.

Through the usual kindness of a wealthy brother, an invitation was accepted to share with himself and wife a western trip to the state of Ohio. They visited a warm-hearted Community friend, and on their return received a cordial welcome. Their experiences abroad were recounted and a group picture of the Inductive Communion, with a small sum of money, was presented to my father, all of which proved very acceptable. The picture is now in the possession of one of the members.

It is proper that I tell you what became of our first-born in Hopedale. Lucy Ballou Lillie went to the West for a short time and later to the South. I have since learned that long ago she passed to the Spirit Land.

Adin Ballou Harris I lost sight of for nearly forty years. Being informed where he was I wrote him and in return received interesting letters from him, giving me great pleasure. He is settled in New Hampton, Iowa, and is a prosperous farmer, an Abstractor of Titles. He has a fine family and some grandchildren. He seems to be a very busy man. In his last correspondence he writes of their early sacrifices and self-denials and of the general aspect of the country on his arrival when a boy, as compared with its present thriving condition, inviting me to visit his "Paradise" as he now deems it. I sent him the history of the Hopedale

Community in which he manifested great interest. The names of several parties were familiar but he could not recall the faces. He alludes to his pleasant childhood, and to playing "Leap Frog" at one of our festivals to the amusement of the company. I think of him as an unusual lad, an adept at figures and a marvel to the school committee. He seems, so far as I know, a worthy follower of the teachings which were so earnestly inculcated in the earliest days of the Community.

Notwithstanding there was much happiness in Community life as a whole, disaffections began to spring up; the spirit of conciliation and forbearance was not always exhibited; human genius began to unfold when least expected. Our original ministers and some laymen gradually began to sigh for the "loaves and fishes" which but a short time before they had exchanged for the new order of society. They had failed to realize either their own imperfections or those of the others. While claiming their principles were mainly the same as ever, they thought times were not ripe for such experiments, and that their dreams were Utopian. So they were pleased to return to the old order of society and to accept their old ways, leaving the founder and a few faithful adherents to fight the battle alone.

Thus have I partially indicated from memory's page the origin and early history of the Hopedale Community. Its greatest crisis took place in 1856 after many changes and governmental transformation adapted to the necessities of the case. But the final act of dissolution was declared December 15, 1873. Thus ended one of the grandest experiments ever attempted for the good of mankind. Seemingly it failed to accomplish what its founder had hoped for, but the seed sown by him and his earnest co-workers for a higher civilization will one day be realized, and a truer, better order of society will then supplant the present disorderly and crude state that exists.

Adin Ballou's faith continued to the end of a long life. He always believed that man would develop into a true nobleness of life and character after the Christ-like pattern of Jesus of Nazareth. That we may be infused with his spirit and that of his faithful co-workers is the sincere wish of
    your friend,
        Abbie Ballou Heywood

Dorchester, Massachusetts

Hopedale

William F. Draper

here are few men identified with the State of Massachusetts who have left a more brilliant record in the line of invention than [my grandfather, Ira Draper]. A native of Dedham, he removed to Weston in 1808, and during his residence there he devoted himself to perfecting the power loom, and finally succeeded in inventing what he styled the "revolving temple" for weaving, which is still manufactured in Hopedale ...

In 1853 [my father, George Draper] removed from Ware to Hopedale ... going into partnership with his brother, E. D. Draper, who was then manufacturing and selling the temples invented by their father, and which he (George) had improved. E. D. Draper was also president of the Hopedale Community, which my father joined, and which I shall refer to later. In 1855 the Hopedale Community came to grief financially, and he joined his brother in paying its debts, which they accomplished within the next few years. From this time his business increased until it has become one of the great manufacturing industries of the State.

He was a man of large inventive capacity and possessed also the business faculty which enabled him to introduce into use his own inventions and those of others, which he controlled, at a profit not only to the community but to himself. The improvements introduced in spinning machinery under his auspices and the writer's have doubled its production and saved to this and foreign countries hundreds of millions of dollars in machinery, and tens of millions per annum in power, labor, and incidentals. He was a total abstainer, a Unitarian in religious belief, never used tobacco, and prior to the War he was a Garrisonian abolitionist. During the war he was an ardent Union man, and worked earnestly for the cause. He organized several companies of volunteers, paying their preliminary expenses and making personal gifts to each man. He was active in recruiting and a member of Governor Andrew's private Advisory Board. After the war he was a thorough and enthusiastic Republican, and an earnest believer in a protective tariff. He founded, and presided over until his death, the celebrated Home Market Club, which crystallizes and represents the protective sentiment of New England. He wrote much on political topics, both in pamphlets and newspaper articles, and no one could fail to understand what he meant, even if he did not agree with him. During the latter years of his life he travelled much, both at home and abroad, giving up to a large extent his business cares. He was active in the formation of the new town of Hopedale in 1886, and built and presented to that town its town hall. His was a strong individuality, and, though he consistently refused public position, he was always a power behind the throne in local and State affairs.

My mother seems to me to have been the very embodiment of New England common sense. Though her life was largely devoted to household duties and the rearing of her children, she was thoroughly interested in public questions, and never satisfied until she had settled to her own satisfaction the right or wrong of anything that came up for consideration. Though my father was a positive man, she was equally sure in her own views – one evidence of which was that though he became a member of the Hopedale Community, she persistently refused to join, on the ground that she did not believe all questions should be settled by a majority vote or that there should be no rewards for pre-eminent ability and services.

Into this village and community of Hopedale I came with my father's family, as a boy of eleven. The change from the ordinary village life to which I was accustomed was marked enough to give me impressions which I remember clearly. The children were under certain community regulations, outside of the usual parental control, among which I remember especially the designation of certain hours for play, and the restriction of amusement to those hours, anywhere outside the domicile of the child's parents. Going to the neighboring town of Milford was discouraged, except in case of emergency, and when we did go we were glad to get back, as the boys there did not sympathize with the Community, and greeted us with opprobrious epithets, if nothing worse. We were sometimes assailed, and if the number were not too great on the other side the Hopedale boys were inclined to depart from the non-resistance principles of their fathers.

In my first year I attended the Community school, – ungraded, – of which Miss Abbie Ballou, (later Mrs. Heywood), was the teacher, and a most excellent one. After this, it being one of the tenets of the Community that boys should be taught to work, I spent three years in manual labor between April 1st and Thanksgiving Day, and attended school only during the winter terms. Two years I was employed by the "garden" branch, in raising vegetables for the Milford market, being expected to hoe my row with the men employed and succeeding fairly well. The year that I was fourteen I went into the machine shop, then under the charge of my uncle, Mr. J. B. Bancroft, and he gave me as good a chance as he could to learn the use of tools, consistent with my doing a fair amount of work. I remember surprising him by doing in a day a certain job which had usually occupied a man of slower motions and less interest an entire week. My performance was later taken as a standard of what ought to be accomplished in a given time.

After leaving the shop I attended the Home School above mentioned a little more than a year, and concluded my schooling just before I was sixteen years old ...

Before continuing I will relate a few personal recollections of the Community regime, which continued in force nearly up to this time. A lyceum was held every Tuesday evening, in which the boys were all interested, and in which, later, some of us took a part. Here were discussed the details of living, as well as general subjects. The question of vegetarianism, as against the use of animal food, was discussed at great length, and the boys were all with the advocates of *meat*. One orator stated that not only should animal food be dispensed with by the truly refined, but that the use of vegetables should be determined by the distance from the ground at which the ripened product was gathered. Potatoes and turnips were of the earth, earthy; cucumbers and squashes were not much better; and he recommended the use of grains which grew several feet from the ground, adding that no doubt as the human race progressed, it would subsist entirely upon fruit. The meat-eating advocate responded, amid the applause of the boys, that nuts, growing still higher, would be a proper food for the gentleman who had last spoken, but he had learned on inquiry that he was one of the greatest meat-eaters in the village. This conviction of inconsistency floored him.

Discussions also covered the use of tea and coffee, and of eggs, which are animal in origin, and some even objected to milk, on the same ground. Dress and the private relations of life were also discussed to our delectation, and there was an evident desire on the part of leading members to regulate living down to the minutest detail. In an annual report of my uncle, as president of the Community, in 1855, he said:

> I think the meetings held of late to discuss matters relating to expenditures and modes of living ... have been and will be productive of much good. When we can come together and talk plainly concerning what we shall eat, drink and wear, – talk of economizing, in a way that shall be understood by those at fault, – and all preserve a loving disposition and maintain a proper self-control, I think it speaks much for our good.

The Sunday meetings were unusual, and sometimes very interesting. There were, I think, five regular preachers, taking turns; and the pulpit was also frequently occupied by eminent men from abroad, including unordained reformers. Among them I distinctly remember William Lloyd Garrison, Wendell Phillips, Stephen S. Foster, Henry C. Wright, and Prof. William Denton. I have been told that Anna Dickinson made her first speech in public in the Hopedale pulpit. After the address, whether from home or outside talent, any listener was allowed to speak or ask questions, and meetings often lasted several hours.

I remember a case in which my father took part. An advocate of Free Love had the pulpit, and delivered an address. My father questioned him, and made an opposing argument, and a vote was taken in which he, (my father), was nearly unanimously sustained. About a month later the same man came again with a similar sermon. My father rose and said we were told to "prove all things and hold fast that which is good," but that if the task of proving the same thing to the same man was to be repeated every month, the labor would become monotonous and little progress would be made. He finished by saying that he thought some foundation principles should be considered as settled, long enough to remember what they were, – and once more he was rewarded by a unanimous assent, and the free lover never appeared there again.

Another incident of another kind, that my mother told me, may be interesting. When we moved to Hopedale, among our household goods were some old-fashioned stuffed parlor chairs, covered with horsehair, such as were in most New England parlors half a century ago. A short time after our arrival my mother received a call from a committee, who lectured her for having such extravagant furniture, when there were so many poor people in the world. Wooden bottomed chairs were pronounced good enough, and I agree that they are more comfortable than the kind criticized. My mother replied that the extravagance of buying them was committed before coming to Hopedale, and the occasion passed with a warning to do so no more. A few years later, after the financial change in the organization, my mother, calling upon one of the former committee, found some modern upholstered chairs and asked why "such extravagant furniture was in use when there were so many poor people in the world." The reply was, "Mrs. Draper, I have changed my mind." It may be fair to say that the party's circumstances had also changed.

My aunt, the wife of the president of the Community, made the mistake of buying an easy chair, which caused a great excitement, until it was agreed that it should be used as a sick chair and sent from house to house for use by invalids, in case of illness, – and that when not so needed, my aunt should be its custodian.

One excellent institution was a Christmas Festival, which was then a much less common observance than it is now. There were addresses by some of the clergy, songs by the musical, pieces spoken by the children, and short plays by the young people, – all being crowned by a Christmas Tree. Those who desired to give presents to members of their families or others brought them to the tree for distribution, and a committee, of whom my mother was one, saw that no man, woman or child of the village went without some remembrance. To those not otherwise provided a handkerchief was given, and at my first Christmas a handkerchief was all that I received. Stocking hanging at home was replaced by the tree, and I remember feeling that communism was a disadvantage as far as I was concerned; especially since most of the other children, and even my younger sisters, had little presents on the tree from their parents. The next year I determined to make a better showing, so I bought a pocket book with some of my farm wages, hung it on the tree for myself, – and received the pocket book *and* a handkerchief. After this my recollection on this point is not clear. I was either better treated or had less feeling about it.

One more anecdote, and I will pass on. In the fifties there was a movement for the reform of women's dress, which consisted in the adoption of a costume designed and first worn by Mrs. Amelia Bloomer. Corsets were abandoned, skirts were shortened to the knee, and supported from the shoulder, while trousers similar to those worn by men, (if I remember aright), completed the costume. As Hopedale was in the front rank in the adoption of real or alleged reforms, several of the ladies temporarily adopted this dress and were regarded as great curiosities when they went outside the "Dale." My mother's mother paid us a visit before she had seen or heard of this innovation, and one day in looking out of the window she saw a dress reformer coming down the street. She called my mother, and pointing to the apparition, said, "Hannah, what is that?"

My mother replied, "That is what we call a Bloomer."

"Is that all?" said my good grandmother; "I thought it might be the Devil."

Memories of the Hopedale Home School

from *Home School Memorial:
A Reunion of Teachers and Pupils of the
Hopedale Home School, August 1, 1867*

Retrospective Sketch

*By the Committee: William F. Draper,
Lizzie B. Humphrey, and William S. Heywood*

he Hopedale Home School was established in the spring of the year 1856, by William S. and Abbie B. Heywood, under whose superintendence, as Principals, it continued during the entire period of its existence. Like the "Collegiate and Classical Institute," started two years previously, of which it was the proper successor, it was a Boarding and Day School, open to pupils of both sexes – its members being about equally divided between the two. It was located in the beautiful village of Hopedale, Milford, Mass., a place easy of access from all parts of the country, and not excelled probably by any in New England, or in the world, for its moral and social advantages, whereby it was rendered peculiarly appropriate for the home of children and youth during those precarious years when they are most endangered by the sins and follies of the world.

The Institution was designed to aid those who might avail themselves of its privileges in the attainment of a thorough, systematic, and practical education, – its leading purpose having been to induct the mind into the principles and elements of all intellectual growth and acquirement – to stimulate self-reliance, the habit and power of thought, patient investigation, dispassionate judgment, freedom of opinion, independence of character, self-culture – to give a true idea of life, and to insure a faithful discharge of life's high duties and sacred trusts.

Its course of study was liberal and comprehensive, giving chief prominence to English scholarship, and, while providing for ample tuition in ancient and modern languages, emphasizing the importance of mathematical studies, and the various departments of natural science to a true and perfect culture. Recognizing the value of the fine arts – music and painting – it furnished facilities for their acquisition. Physical training and the laws of health received attention, theoretically and practically, while all was regarded as subordinate to that moral and spiritual nurture and instruction which was employed to develop and establish pure, virtuous, exalted characters – thus moulding and confirming the noblest types of Christian manhood and womanhood.

The school year of forty weeks was divided into three terms: two of fifteen weeks each, and one of ten weeks, commencing respectively on the first Wednesdays of September, January, and May. Public examinations were held at the close of the winter term in April, and public exhibitions given at the end of the autumn term in December. A daily notation of the deportment and fidelity of each pupil was kept, constituting the basis of a report made to parents and guardians at the close of each term. A small but well-chosen library was connected with the Institution, and also apparatus for illustrating the natural sciences.

The School continued for seven years, until 1863, when the Principals, for various reasons, were induced to give it up, and no one appearing to assume their responsibilities, it was permanently closed.

Such is a brief outline of the history of the Hopedale Home School. It is to be hoped and believed that it answered in some good degree the end for which it was established, not only giving, according to its means, thorough instruction in the various branches of intellectual culture, but helping to make true and worthy men and women – the noblest product of any clime. Its day was brief, but the assurances are many and strong that it wrought a good work in its time – that it gave to many minds useful knowledge, quickened in many souls high and noble impulses and purposes of good – that it linked many hearts in the bonds of a deep and sacred friendship – that it

> Deposited on the silent shores
> Of memory, images and precious thoughts
> That cannot die, that cannot be destroyed.

ADDRESS BY THE ORATOR OF THE DAY
Arnold B. Chase

Ladies and Gentlemen, – Schoolmates, I would rather call you, for, as I look around me here, I see many a well-remembered face, – we are met today to renew our olden friendships, and to call back to memory the days of our school-life passed together. For a few short hours, "The Home School" exists again, so vivid and real are the scenes and associations which this day brings to mind. We almost fancy ourselves back in jackets and short dresses, conning once more our tasks in yonder schoolroom.

How many are the incidents, long since passed out of mind, which today come back in throngs! Once more the hearty laugh fills yonder room, as the long arms of our teacher bear down upon us in the game of "Blind man's buff." Once more the boys' sitting-room echoes with the crash of chairs, that are used for footballs. Once more the signal sounds in yonder attics, and all is quiet, save the deep breathing of the sleeping ones, where, but a moment before, pillows were throwing, and doors were slamming, in some youthful frolic. We feel again all the excitement of our exhibitions, and all the dread of our examinations. We remember today both the wild freaks of our boyish thoughtlessness, and the acts of our sober hours, when we tried to do our best, – our insane desire to do that which was forbidden, as well as our earnest desire to do our duty.

Response to Toast
"To the Principals of the Home School"
Summary of remarks by William S. Heywood

Mr. Heywood ... proceeded to indulge in reminiscences and retrospections, calling up many scenes forgotten and unforgotten by others, narrating many incidents and occurrences that took place while he was Principal of the Home School. He cited illustrations of both the pleasures and pains of his experience, in both the domestic and educational departments of the Institution, not forgetting to allude to the "Public Examinations," to which the Pupils usually came with so much fear and trembling, through which they usually passed with so much credit; and to the "Public Exhibitions," which were always taken hold of with so much enthusiasm, and carried through with so much success.

Referring to the remark of the Orator of the Day concerning the "crashing of chairs" and "slamming of doors" and "rending of bedding," he said "he felt the damaging effects of some of those exercises of youthful exuberance in the nerve of his pocket to this day." His account of the "candy party," in which, on a certain time, he caught some eight or ten of his "first class" pupils locked into a little out of-the-way-room, eating candy made of molasses surreptitiously procured by them from his own barrel, and not yet, he believed, paid for, produced considerable merriment.

As also did the story of the young man who, deprived of all educational opportunities in his earlier life, came to the School, from an Overseership in a factory, in order to gratify his earnest desire for self-improvement. Narrating to Mr. H., on the evening of his arrival, some events in his experience, he ingenuously stated that some of the operatives under him had become so attached to him, as to be moved to tears upon his leaving them. After he retired for the night, several of the principal young ladies of the School, who had overheard the conversation, laughed at it, and said, contemptuously, "Wonder if we shall shed any tears when he goes away from here!"

"And yet, if you will believe it," said Mr. H., "when that young man did go away, after only a few months' stay, every one of those young ladies did shed tears, and in good earnest, too. Nor was it at all to their discredit, for that young man proved to be one of the most worthy persons who ever attended the Home School, endearing himself, while there, not only to the young ladies, but to all who knew him, by his personal virtues and Christian spirit."

Catalogue of the Hopedale Home School

from *Home School Memorial:*
A Reunion of Teachers and Pupils of the
Hopedale Home School, August 1, 1867

The asterisk (*) indicates those present at the Reunion; the dagger (†) those deceased by 1867. Names assumed by marriage after leaving the School are in parentheses.

Board of Instructors

	Name	Position	Residence in 1867
*	William S. Heywood	Principal	Hudson, MA
*	Abbie B. Heywood	Associate Principal	Hudson, MA
	George S. Dickinson	Teacher of French	Milford, MA
	Lucy B. Whitney	Assistant Teacher	Westminster, MA
*	Mary A. Read	Assistant Teacher	Boston.MA
	H. Amanda Albee (Stafford)	Assistant Teacher	Albany, NY
*	Lizzie B. Humphrey	Assistant Teacher	Hopedale
	Sophia L. Bloom	Teacher of Music	Hoboken, NJ
	Prof. O. B. Young	Teacher of Music	Lansing, MI
	Lucy B. Whitney	Teacher of Music	Westminster, MA
	Prof. A. W. Bailey	Teacher of Music	
*	Esther A. Read	Matron	Hopedale
*	Adelia L. Heywood	Matron	Milford, MA
	Mary A. Wells	Matron	Wilbraham, MA
*	J. Lowell Heywood	Steward	Milford, MA

Pupils

	Name	Home Town	Residence in 1867
*	Adams, Addie C. (Marsh)	Hopedale	Providence, RI
*	Adams, Lizzie	Hopedale	Hopedale
*	Adams, Moses C.	Medfield, MA	Medfield, MA
†	Adams, Warren L.	Hopedale	
	Albee, Clarence	Milford, MA	Milford, MA

Catalogue of the Hopedale Home School 75

	Name	Home Town	Residence in 1867
	Albee, H. Amanda (Stafford)	Hopedale	Albany, NY
*	Albee, Ida D.	Hopedale	Hopedale
*	Alden, Hattie E. (Barber)	Milford, MA	Milford, MA
	Alderman, Alice (Hook)	Framingham	Boston, MA
†	Alderman, Charles	Framingham, MA	
	Alderman, Frank F.	Framingham, MA	Boston, MA
	Aldrich, Frank	Mendon, MA	Boston, MA
	Allen, Etta B.	Sturbridge, MA	Milwaukee, WI
	Allen, Frank	Milford, MA	Milford, MA
	Ambler, Charles	Milford, MA	Milford, MA
	Ames, M. Eugene	Salem, MA	
*	Atkins, George D.	Florence, MA	New York, NY
	Bachelor, George W.	Milford, MA	Milford, MA
†	Ball, Eli G.	Hopedale	
	Ballou, Austin	Milford, MA	
*	Bancroft, Eben D.	Hopedale	Hopedale
*	Bancroft, Willie	Hopedale	Hopedale
*	Banks, Sarah A.	Providence, RI	Providence, RI
	Bartlett, Lucy A.	Milford, NH	Milford, NH
†	Barton, Vesta A.	Milford, MA	
	Beal, D. Francis	Hopedale	Illinois
	Beal, Rufus	Hopedale	Hopedale
*	Belcher, Luther, Jr.	Stoughton, MA	Stoughton, MA
	Bemis, Melvin	Hopedale	Hudson, MA
	Bennett, Herbert	Mendon, MA	Mendon, MA
	Bennett, Mary A.	Hopedale	Gloucester, MA
†	Blake, Anna	Hopedale	
	Blake, Isabel	Hopedale	San Francisco, CA
	Booth, Sarah J.	Newark, IL	Newark, IL
	Bowker, John E.	Milford, MA	Boston, MA
*	Boyden, Mary E.	Mendon, MA	Mendon, MA
	Boynton, Richard	O'Fallan, IL	St. Louis, MO
*	Bradbury, Sarah E.	Hopedale	Hopedale
*	Bragg, John F.	Braggville, MA	Milford, MA
	Bragg, William F.	Braggville, MA	New York, NY
	Brewer, Freddie	Milford, MA	Philadelphia, PA
	Brigham, Mary A. (Pierson)	Milford, MA	Charlestown, MA
*	Brown, Frank G.	Boston, MA	Boston, MA
	Bryan, Sarah J. (Balcom)	Milford, MA	Sterling, IL
	Buffum, Adaline C.	Orono, ME	Chicago, IL
	Buffum, J. Whittier	Orono, ME	Chicago, IL
	Burnham, Chester	Windham, CT	Hartford, CT
*	Burnham, Joseph B.	Boston, MA	Boston, MA
	Burr, Calvin C.	Bellingham, MA	Bellingham, MA

	Name	Home Town	Residence in 1867
	Butterworth, Alice	Bellingham, MA	
†	Callum, Gilbert	Bellingham, MA	
	Campbell, Anna C.	New York, NY	New York, NY
	Carpenter, Marion	Milford, MA	Milford, MA
	Carpenter, William	Upton, MA	Lake Superior
†	Carter, Oscar H.	Hopedale	
*	Cary, Addie M.	Medway, MA	Medway, MA
	Cassey, Francis L.	Salem, MA	Detroit, MI
	Cerren, William H.	Milford, MA	New York, NY
	Chapin, Edwin	Milford, MA	Milford, MA
	Chapin, Willard	Milford, MA	Milford, MA
*	Chapman, Ada W.	Mystic, CT	Hopedale
*	Chapman, Alice B.	Hopedale	Hopedale
	Chapman, Anna C.	Richmond, MA	Richmond, MA
	Chapman, Eva L.	Hopedale	Providence, RI
†	Chapman, H. Amelia	Hopedale	
*	Chapman, Mary A. (Davenport)	Mystic, CT	Mendon, MA
*	Chapman, N. Everett	Mystic, CT	Hopedale
*	Chapman, Nettie W.	Mystic, CT	Hopedale
*	Chase, Arnold B.	Valley Falls, RI	Valley Falls, RI
†	Chase, Samuel O.	Valley Falls, RI	
	Cheever, Charles H.	Boston, MA	Boston, MA
*	Cheever, Joseph	Portsmouth, NH	Portsmouth, NH
	Cheney, Almon	Milford, MA	Milford, MA
	Cheney, Edwin	Milford, MA	Milford, MA
	Child, Lizzie N.	Philadelphia, PA	Philadelphia, PA
	Chilson, Addie (Warfield)	Bellingham, MA	
	Chilson, Ellen (Chilson)	Bellingham, MA	
	Church, Edward H.	E. Killingly, CT	
*	Claflin, Estelle S.	Milford, MA	Milford, MA
*	Claflin, Waldo L.	Milford, MA	New York, NY
	Clapp, Rollin H.	Montague, MA	Montague, MA
*	Clark, Charles E.	Milford, MA	Milford, MA
	Clark, Lucy M.	Milford, MA	Milford, MA
	Clark, Ransom J.	Milford, MA	Milford, MA
	Clark, William C.	Milford, MA	Milford, MA
	Clarke, Arthur M.	Hopedale	Providence, RI
	Clarke, Frank	Providence, RI	Oskaloosa, IA
	Cleveland, Kate H.	Brooklyn, NY	
	Colby, J. Harlan	Amesbury, MA	
	Coleman, Augusta	Mendon, MA	
	Comstock, Ada	Woonsocket, RI	

Catalogue of the Hopedale Home School   77

	Name	Home Town	Residence in 1867
	Comstock, Angela S.	Woonsocket, RI	
	Comstock, Daniel W.	Milford, MA	Mendon, MA
	Connor, Caty	Milford, MA	Milford, MA
*	Cook, Agnes L. (Thayer)	Blackstone, MA	Milford, MA
	Cook, Alfred	Milford, MA	Milford, MA
	Cook, Alonzo S.	Milford, MA	Milford, MA
*	Cook, Angelia	Milford, MA	Milford, MA
	Cook, Byron S.	Providence, RI	Providence, RI
*	Cook, Christopher	Milford, MA	Milford, MA
	Cook, Edward	Mendon, MA	Milford, MA
	Cook, Edward E.	Milford, MA	Milford, MA
	Cook, Halsey	Milford, MA	Hopedale
	Cook, Ira B.	Bellingham, MA	
	Cook, James S.	Bellingham, MA	
	Cook, Orville	Danvers, MA	Milford, MA
*	Cook, Revilo	Danvers, MA	Milford, MA
	Cook, Solon	Milford, MA	Milford, MA
	Cooney, Timothy	Milford, MA	Milford, MA
	Crosby, Artemas B.	Groton, NH	
	Daniels, Augustus	Milford, MA	Milford, MA
*	Daniels, Willie	Milford, MA	Milford, MA
†	Darling, Austin	Nasonville, RI	
	Davenport, Austin D.	Mendon, MA	Mendon, MA
	Davenport, John E.	Mendon, MA	Mendon, MA
	Davenport, Rebecca (Cummings}	Mendon, MA	Boston, MA
	Davenport, Seth T.	Mendon, MA	Milford, MA
*	Davenport, Stearns G.	Mendon, MA	Mendon, MA
	Delanah, Abby P. (Prescott)	Providence, RI	Rochester, NY
	Dempsey, Joseph	Milford, MA	Milford, MA
	Dempsey, Martin	Milford, MA	Milford, MA
	Denny, Clark K.	Clappville, MA	Watertown, MA
	Denny, Frank D.	Clappville, MA	Watertown, MA
	Denny, Thomas	Clappville, MA	Watertown, MA
	Despeau, Gardner	Milford, MA	Mendon, MA
	Despeau, O. Trask	Milford, MA	Boston, MA
	Dodge, Charles	Milford, MA	
	Downing, Serena A. M. (Washington)	Newport, RI	Newport, RI
	Drake, Elizabeth B.	Bellingham, MA	
*	Draper, Annetta	Hopedale	Hopedale
*	Draper, Fannie E.	Hopedale	Hopedale
*	Draper, Hannah T.	Hopedale	Hopedale

Home School Memorial

Name	Home Town	Residence in 1867
* Draper, Mary A.	Hopedale	Hopedale
* Draper, Oscar E.	Hopedale	Hopedale
* Draper, William F.	Hopedale	Hopedale
Dunbar, James A.	Carlisle, PA	Carlisle, PA
Dunn, Moses L.	Milford, MA	Mendon, MA
* Dutcher, Frank J.	Hopedale	Hopedale
Eldridge, Lydia A.	Milford, MA	Milford, MA
Ellis, Charles	Milford, MA	Worcester, MA
* Ellis, Ella E.	Mendon, MA	Mendon, MA
Ellis, Henrietta	Milford, MA	Milford, MA
Ellsworth, Mary	Milford, MA	Milford, MA
Everett, Emma C. (Howe)	Princeton, MA	San Francisco, CA
Fales, Susan	Milford, MA	Milford, MA
† Farr, Edwards D.	Leicester, MA	
Fish, Charles H.	Hopedale	Gloucester, MA
Fish, Margaret E.	Hopedale	Gloucester, MA
* Fish, William H., Jr.	Cortland, NY	Cambridge, MA
* Fisher, L. Laurene	W. Wrentham, MA	W. Wrentham, MA
Fisher, Victoria L.	Cordaville, MA	
* Fiske, Edwards D.	Milford, MA	Brooklyn, NY
* Ford, George R.	Mendon, MA	Mendon, MA
Gardner, George	Boston, MA	Boston, MA
Garnet, Henry	New York, NY	New York, NY
Garnet, Mary H.	New York, NY	New York, NY
* Gaskill, Julia E.	Mendon, MA	Mendon, MA
* Gay, Marianna	Hopedale	Chelsea, MA
Gloucester, Lizzie	Brooklyn, NY	
* Godfrey, Annie R.	Milford, MA	Milford, MA
Godfrey, Stearns	Milford, MA	Milford, MA
Godfrey, Wilson	Steuben, ME	
† Goldsmith, Ellen M.	Milford, MA	
Goldsmith, M. Lizzie	Milford, MA	Milford, MA
Googins, Abby	Milford, MA	Boston, MA
Goss, Ellen E.	Mendon, MA	Mendon, MA
Goss, Lewis P.	Mendon, MA	Worcester, MA
Grant, A. Orville	Medway, MA	
Grant, Elbridge	Bellingham, MA	
Grant, Emory	Milford, MA	Milford, MA
Greason, James D.	Carlisle, PA	Dayton, OH
Greason, John H.	Carlisle, PA	Wilkins, PA
Greene, Alonzo	Boston, MA	Dover, NH
Greene, Charles G.	Hopedale	Lonsdale, RI
Greene, Sarah		

Catalogue of the Hopedale Home School 79

	Name	Home Town	Residence in 1867
	Greene, William B.	Gloversville, NY	
	Hale, Sarah (Woodbury)	Berlin, MA	Berlin, MA
	Hall, Isaiah	Hopedale	
*	Hall, Mary E.	Grafton, MA	Grafton, MA
*	Harlow, Henry	Hopedale	Hopedale
*	Harlow, Joseph W.	Hopedale	Hopedale
*	Hartles, Mary A. (Trevett)	Hopedale	Hopedale
	Haskell, Cyrus A.	Lowell, MA	Gloucester, MA
*	Hastings, Annie W. (Pierce)	Mendon, MA	Mendon, MA
*	Hastings, George E.	Milford, MA	Milford, MA
	Hastings, Ruby W. (Sumner)	Milford, MA	Watertown, MA
	Hastings, William S.	Milford, MA	Milford, MA
	Hawes, Albert E.	W. Wrentham, MA	Boston, MA
*	Hayden, Fannie E. (Talbot)	Pembroke, ME	Eastport, ME
	Hayden, Lewis	Milford, MA	Milford, MA
	Hero, Ada P.	Milford, MA	Milford, MA
*	Hero, Cora A. (Mayhew)	Milford, MA	Milford, MA
*	Heywood, Charles H.	Westminster, MA	New Berne, NC
*	Heywood, Stella W.	Hopedale	Hudson, MA
	Higgins, Katy	Milford, MA	
	Hilton, George G.	Salem, MA	Boston, MA
	Hixon, Charles	Milford, MA	Milford, MA
	Holbrook, J. W.	Upton, MA	Upton, MA
	Howe, Nathan	Milford, MA	Hopkinton, MA
	Howe, Stedman	Milford, MA	Milford, MA
	Howe, Willard	Milford, MA	Milford, MA
*	Humphrey, Lizzie B.	Hopedale	Hopedale
	Hunt, Edwin	Milford, MA	Milford, MA
*	Hunt, Pearley M.	Milford, MA	Milford, MA
	Huntoon, Emma	Milford, MA	Milford, MA
	Hutchinson, Justin E.	Milford, NH	Amherst, NH
*	Ide, Sarah E. (Symonds)	Milford, MA	Milford, MA
*	Inman, Asa F.	Hopedale	Milford, MA
	Jackson, Charles F.	Boston, MA	Boston, MA
	Johnson, Arabella	Reed's Ferry, NH	
†	Johnson, Charles	Hopedale	
	Johnson, Hannah (Hurd)	Sturbridge, MA	Dansville, NY
†	Johnson, J. Arthur	Sturbridge, MA	
	Johnson, Julia B. (Dillaby)	Milford, MA	Norwich, CT
	Johnson, Katy (Jackson)	Sturbridge, MA	Dansville, NY
*	Johnson, Norman	Hopkinton, MA	Boston, MA
*	Joy, Lilla (Draper)	Hopedale	Hopedale
	Keith, Josie L. (Sinclair)	Worcester, MA	Wisconsin

	Name	Home Town	Residence in 1867
	Kelly, Lucina	Blackstone, MA	Blackstone, MA
	Kinsley, William S.	Mendon, MA	Mendon, MA
	Lanigan, Ann	Milford, MA	
	Lanigan, Luke	Milford, MA	Milford, MA
	Lewers, Mary W. (Crouch)	Hopedale	Mystic, CT
	Lewers, Nancy W.	Hopedale	Hopedale
	Lillie, Lucy B. (Darrah)	Hopedale	California
	Lillie, Sarah P.	Hopedale	California
†	Ludden, Alonzo	Brooklyn, NY	
	Ludden, William A.	Brooklyn, NY	New York, NY
	Madden, Amos L.	Milford, MA	Hopkinton, MA
	Madden, Sylvester L.	Milford, MA	Milford, MA
	Magoun, Frank L.	E. Cambridge, MA	E. Cambridge, MA
	Main, C. Wesley	Boston, MA	
	Marsh, George W.	Mendon, MA	Providence, RI
*	Mascroft, Imogene W.	Northbridge, MA	Rockdale, MA
	Mathewson, Frank E.	Milford, MA	Milford, MA
*	Mathewson, William A.	Milford, MA	Milford, MA
*	May, George P.	Dorchester, MA	Dorchester, MA
*	Mayhew, John S.	Milford, MA	Milford, MA
	Mead, Edward B.	Milford, MA	Milford, MA
	Mead, George J.	Milford, MA	Meadville, PA
	Mellen, John B.	Mendon, MA	Mendon, MA
	Metcalf, Charles	Milford, MA	Milford, MA
	Metcalf, George	Milford, MA	Milford, MA
†	Miller, Alice	Mendon, MA	
†	Moore, Ellen M.	Hopedale	
	Mowry, Lewellyn	Milford, MA	Milford, MA
	Mulliken, Helen E.	Hopedale	Phenix, RI
	Munroe, George A.	Plainfield, CT	
†	Munroe, Hattie A.	Plainfield, CT	
	Munroe, Nancy M. (Stratton)	Plainfield, CT	
*	Munyan, Anna G. (Warren)	Phenix, RI	Providence, RI
	Munyan, Catharine G.	Hopedale	Providence, RI
	Murphy, Dennis	Milford, MA	
	Murphy, Edward	Milford, MA	
	Murphy, Patrick	Milford, MA	
*	Nason, George G.	Milford, MA	New York, NY
	Nason, Henry	Milford, MA	New York, NY
*	Nelson, Ellen M.	Milford, MA	Milford, MA
	Nelson, Livy (Vant)	Milford, MA	Milford, MA
*	Nelson, Mary E. (Brown)	Milford, MA	Milford, MA

Catalogue of the Hopedale Home School 81

	Name	Home Town	Residence in 1867
	Nelson, Sarah E. (Doggett)	Milford, MA	Milford, MA
	Newcomb, Hannah A.	S. Reading, MA	S. Reading, MA
	Newell, Josephine A.	Boston, MA	
	Noyes, Idella R. (Clark)	Milford, MA	Fitchburg, MA
*	Noyes, Mary L.	Milford, MA	Milford, MA
	Parke, Alice M.	Brooklyn, MA	
*	Patrick, Henry L.	Hopedale	Hopedale
	Pease, Lucia D. (Ellis)	S. Wilbraham, MA	S. Wilbraham, MA
	Peck, Frank E.	Bellingham, MA	Boston, MA
	Perham, Sarah	Mendon, MA	Mendon, MA
†	Perry, George L.	Hopedale	
	Phelps, George T.	Harvard, MA	Springfield, MA
*	Pond, A. V. G.	Mendon, MA	Woonsocket, RI
†	Pond, Henry	Milford, MA	
	Pratt, Willie A.	Providence, RI	Chelsea, MA
*	Purvis Sarah M.	Bridgewater, PA	Philadelphia, PA
	Rawson, Charles H.	Mendon, MA	Mendon, MA
	Rawson, Medora A. (Davenport)	Mendon, MA	Mendon, MA
	Ray, Edgar	Bellingham, MA	Bellingham, MA
*	Read, Mary A.	Hopedale	Boston, MA
*	Rice, George	Newport, RI	Dartmouth College, NH
*	Rice, Lucy	Boston, MA	Boston, MA
	Rich, Gilbert	Braggville, MA	Milford, MA
	Richardson, Henry S.	Medfield, MA	Medfield, MA
	Roberts, Warren L.	S. Danvers, MA	
	Rockwood, Aaron W.	Milford, MA	Milford, MA
	Rockwood, Jotham	Milford, MA	Milford, MA
	Rogers, Charles B.	Waterbury, CT	
	Rounds, Mary E. (Bradbury)	Milford, MA	Milford, MA
	Russell, E. Charles	Toledo, OH	
	Russell, Edgar	Milford, MA	
	Russell, Jane	Milford, MA	Milford, MA
	Sargent, C. Henry	S. Reading, MA	
	Saunders, Jonathan B.	Milford, MA	Milford, MA
*	Scott, Emma	Hopedale	Bellingham, MA
	Scott, Emma L.	Hopedale	Cuba, NY
*	Scott, Frances E.	Hopedale	Bellingham, MA
	Scott, Mary E. (Tebb)	Hopedale	England
	Sheldon, Charles	Randolph, NY	
	Shepard, Lewis C.	Milford, MA	Milford, MA
	Shove, Frank S.	Pawtucket, RI	California
	Smith, Samuel W.	Brooklyn, NY	

	Name	Home Town	Residence in 1867
	Southwick, Andre A.	Millville, MA	Blackstone, MA
	Southwick, George H.	Millville, MA	Worcester, MA
	Southworth, Alvah F.	Milford, MA	Hardwick, MA
	Southworth, C. Eugene	Milford, MA	Hardwick, MA
	Southworth, Oscar	Milford, MA	Hardwick, MA
	Staples, H. Benton	Mendon, MA	Mendon, MA
	Staples, Sarah L.	Mendon, MA	Mendon, MA
	Sterritt, John	Blackstone, MA	
*	Stevens, Hattie L.	North Andover, MA	Hopedale
	Steward, Frances O.	Mendon, MA	Framingham, MA
	Steward, Ira B.	Hopedale	Boston, MA
	Stimpson, Edward L.	Hopedale	Hopedale
	Stimpson, Joseph	Hopedale	Worcester, MA
	Strain, Edward	Hopedale	
	Stratton, Schuyler	Foxboro, MA	
	Taft, Delia W. (Davenport)	Mendon, MA	Mendon, MA
	Taft, Edward A.	Hopedale	Grafton, MA
	Taft, Edward A.	W. Needham, MA	Boston, MA
	Taft, Frances M. (Mesa)	Hopedale	Rome, GA
	Taft, Frank A.	Mendon, MA	Mendon, MA
	Taft, Sarah Ellen (Finney)	Hopedale	Dalton, GA
	Taylor, Edward L.	Boston, MA	Boston, MA
*	Thayer, Charles	Milford, MA	Milford, MA
*	Thayer, George	Milford, MA	Milford, MA
†	Thayer, Gustavus	Milford, MA	
	Thayer, Marietta (Dewey)	Milford, MA	Milford, MA
	Thayer, Otis Elwood	Mendon, MA	Connecticut
	Thompson, Gilbert	Hopedale	Washington, DC
	Thompson, Willie	Milford, MA	Milford, MA
*	Thwing, Anna	Hopedale	Hopedale
*	Thwing, Susan E. (Whitney)	Hopedale	Hopedale
*	Tilton, Angela F. (Heywood)	Worcester, MA	Worcester, MA
	Tompkins, Serena	Brooklyn, NY	
	Toohey, Patrick	Milford, MA	Milford, MA
	Tourtellot, Georgianna (Warren)	Milford, MA	Wrentham, MA
	Townsend, Keturah	Flushing, NY	
	Usher, Ella M.	Milford, MA	Milford, MA
	Vant, Dexter	Milford, MA	Milford, MA
	Walcott, George	Milford, MA	Westminster, MA
	Walden, Lucy (Adams)	Mendon, MA	Mendon, MA
	Walden, Mary A. (Hagar)	Hopedale	Monticello, MN
	Walden, Susan	Mendon, MA	Mendon, MA

Catalogue of the Hopedale Home School 83

	Name	Home Town	Residence in 1867
*	Walker, Ellen (Gifford)	Hopedale	Hopedale
*	Walker, H. Abby	Milford, MA	Milford, MA
*	Walker, Henrietta	Milford, MA	Milford, MA
	Walpole, Joseph	Boston, MA	
	Warren, C. Harry	Claremont, NH	New York, NY
	Warren, George	Mendon, MA	Upton, MA
	Watson, Burnham K.	Concord, NH	Lakeland, MN
*	Webb, Ada	Milford, MA	Milford, MA
*	Webb, Emma A.	Milford, MA	Milford, MA
	Weeden, Caroline	Boston, MA	
*	Welch, William	Woonsocket, RI	Woonsocket, RI
	Wells, Mary K.	Wilbraham, MA	Wilbraham, MA
	Wheeler, George M.	Hopkinton, MA	California
*	Wheelock, Mary L. (Marsh)	Mendon, MA	Mendon, MA
*	Whipple, Content	Ledyard, CT	Ledyard, CT
*	Whipple, Pamelia	Ledyard, CT	Hopedale
*	Whipple, Sarah (Spofford)	Ledyard, CT	Milford, MA
	Whitney, George	Hopkinton, MA	
	Whitney, Lucy B.	Westminster, MA	Westminster, MA
*	Whitney, Sarah B.	Westminster, MA	Worcester, MA
	Whitney, William	Medway, MA	
	Wiggins, Ella	Ashland, MA	Ashland, MA
	Wilkinson, Mary L.	Milford, MA	Milford, MA
†	Williams, Mary A.	Sheldonville, MA	
	Wilmarth, Jerome	Hopedale	Upton, MA
*	Wilmarth, Phila O. (Weston)	Hopedale	Brooklyn, NY
	Wilson, Annie M.	Brooklyn, NY	
	Wing, Henry T.	Uxbridge, MA	
	Winslow, Marietta	Lynn, MA	
	Wood, Frederick	Milford, MA	Milford, MA
	Wood, Henry	Mendon, MA	Woonsocket, RI
	Wood, Warren	Mendon, MA	Mendon, MA
*	Wyman, Mary A.	Westminster, MA	Westminster, MA
*	Wyman, Sarah J.	Westminster, MA	Westminster, MA
*	Young, George H.	Hopedale	Westford, MA

Adin Ballou   *Lucy Hunt Ballou*

The Old House

Illustrations

Susan Thwing Whitney

Anna Thwing Field

The "Hopedale Penny Post" stamp

The Thwing house, site of the Hopedale post office

The Humphrey house, scene of "The Burglary"

The original Community schoolhouse-chapel, where "Miss Abbie" Ballou taught the district school

Illustrations

Abbie Ballou Heywood and William S. Heywood co-principals of the Hopedale Home School

The two male contributors, Frank J. Dutcher and William F. Draper

www.ingramcontent.com/pod-product-compliance
Lightning Source LLC
Chambersburg PA
CBHW050602300426
44112CB00013B/2042